23

D0820548

Advance Praise for (P)LUCK

"The behind-the-scenes story of how twin brothers—doctor and lawyer—collaborated with scores of unsung heroes to modernize emergency medical services, help create the physician assistant profession, help write the model law for organ donation and develop other programs that save thousands of lives a year. (P)LUCK is an inspiring model for how to lead major change—a great read, couldn't put it down."

—James A Guest
Past President and CEO of Consumer Reports

"An inspirational story of meaningful work devoted to public service, health, and wellbeing. Blair, a lawyer, and Fred, a physician, make the decision to work as a medical-legal team, even before they are quite sure where their talents can be most useful. They end up playing a significant role in establishing the national approach to organ donation, addressing critical shortages in the U.S healthcare workforce, establishing the new profession of physician assistants, contributing to the young field of bioethics, and building the nation's emergency medical response capability."

—Mildred Solomon, EdD
President, The Hastings Center

"They reverse engineer their effectiveness . . . in a series of lessons learned offering guidance for the leadership of change, always emphasizing initiative, optimism, resilience, and above all, cooperation. . . . No matter which of their several quests they describe, Blair and Fred also reveal a level of agility and creativity that marks the best leaders. They always seem to find a pathway out of paralysis and conflict into shared possibility."

—From the Foreword by Donald M. Berwick, MD
President Emeritus and Senior Fellow
Institute for Healthcare Improvement

"A jewel of a book full of keen insight about humane purpose, perseverance, and the power of TWO in making a lasting difference in service to others."

—Leonard L. Berry
University Distinguished Professor of Marketing
Texas A&M University

"I love this book and it should be required reading for all, including students. The fifteen ideas for catalyzing change can bring out the best in all of us. Read it today and plan for your future!"

—Maureen Bisognano
President Emerita and Senior Fellow
Institute for Healthcare Improvement

"A great story, very readable and well written, with lessons for us all."

—Lord Nigel Crisp
Chief Executive, National Health Service, England 2000–2006

"This book is full of gems on how to scale a brilliant idea into widespread adoption. The Sadler brothers have had a major impact on the health sector over the past fifty years. This is their story."

—Gary Cohen,
Cofounder and President, Health Care without Harm

"The authors meticulously and smoothly trace the development of one of the Uniform Law Commission's most important contributions to our country. The reader cannot escape the conclusion that we Uniform law Commissioners know well: our work cannot achieve optimum impact without the thoughtful input from experts, practitioners, and relevant interest groups who will be affected by our model laws."

—Howard J. Swibel
Past President, Uniform Law Commission
Chair, Uniform Law Foundation

"The Sadler brothers were there at the beginning, shaping the early days of bioethics and drafting seminal legislation governing organ transplantation. In this charming account, they demonstrate how individuals can make a difference, offering a wise prescription for a new generation of leadership."

—Joseph J. Fins, MD
Professor of Medical Ethics and Professor of Medicine
Weill Cornell Medical College

"The authors demonstrate how the repeated sharing of ideas in a transparent manner can increase the investment of others in the need for change and affect the lives of many Americans."

—Carl Fasser
Past President, Physician Assistant Education Association
Professor and Program Director, PA Program Baylor College of Medicine

"The authors provide a first-hand account of the early days of the Robert Wood Johnson Foundation as a national philanthropy. They also describe the design, launch, and evaluation of the Foundation's very first national program focused on regional emergency medical communications systems, which served as a prototype for much of the Foundation's grantmaking for many years."

—Calvin Bland
Former Chief of Staff and Special Advisor
The Robert Wood Johnson Foundation

"In this comprehensive report of their journey to enhance health care for the public good, the Sadlers have captured the worth and value of teamwork. The lessons learned are shared for all of us who aspire to improve relationships in our work."

—Loretta C. Ford, PNP, EdD,
Cofounder of the first Nurse Practitioner Program in 1965
University of Colorado

"The authors' stories challenge and empower us to identify comparable decisions and opportunities in our own lives. This book inspires and equips."

—Megan Mayer - author, retired lawyer, Chair, Network for Impact

"This book is a testament to (P)luck—risk taking, teamwork, persistence, creativity, and luck. Their lessons learned provide very valuable wisdom gained from decades of life in the trenches, with skin in the game."

—Donald Pedersen PhD, PA
Past President of the Physician Assistant Education Association and
Past Director of the University of Utah Medex PA Program.

"Over the course of five decades, Fred and Blair Sadler have virtually defined synergism in their pursuit of worthwhile goals. From early on in their careers, they parlayed serendipitous encounters and bold actions that took them into numerous important "rooms where it happened"—resulting in laws, movements, and novel career pathways that changed America's healthcare system for the better."

—Laurence H. Beck, MD, Adjunct Professor of Medicine; University of
Pennsylvania Perelman School of Medicine

(P)LUCK

Other books by the authors:

Alfred M. Sadler, Jr., Blair L. Sadler, and Ann A. Bliss, *The Physician's Assistant—Today and Tomorrow* (New Haven: Yale University Press, 1972).

Alfred M. Sadler, Jr., Blair L. Sadler, and Ann A. Bliss, *The Physician's Assistant—Today and Tomorrow: Issues Confronting New Health Practitioners*, 2nd edition. (Pensacola, FL: Ballinger, 1975). https://pahx.org/wp-content/uploads/2016/11/Sadler_Sadler_Bliss_2nd_Edition.pdf

Alfred M. Sadler, Jr., Blair L. Sadler, and Samuel B. Webb, Jr, *Emergency Medical Care: The Neglected Public Service.* (Cambridge, MA: Ballinger Publishing Co., 1977).

Thomas E. Piemme, Alfred M. Sadler, Jr., Reginald D. Carter, and Ruth Ballweg, *The Physician Assistant: An Illustrated History* (Gilbert, AZ: Acacia Publishing, 2013). pahx.org/pa-history-book/

(P)LUCK

Lessons We Learned for
Improving Healthcare
and the World

Alfred Sadler & Blair Sadler

SILICON
VALLEY
PRESS

Copyright © 2022 Alfred Sadler & Blair Sadler
All rights reserved.

ISBNs: 9781735873176 (hc); 9798985842807 (pbk); 9781735873183 (ebook)
Library of Congress Number: 2022903822

Cover design by Jonathan Bush
Book design by Mayfly Design

SILICON
VALLEY
PRESS

*It is not the critic who counts; not the
man who points out how the strong man
stumbles, or where the doer of deeds could
have done them better.
The credit belongs to the man who is
actually in the arena, whose face is marred by dust
and sweat and blood; who strives valiantly;
who errs, who comes short again and again,
because there is no effort without error
and shortcoming; but who does actually
strive to do the deeds; who knows great
enthusiasms, the great devotions; who spends
himself in a worthy cause; who at the best knows in
the end the triumph of high achievement, and who
at the worst, if he fails, at least fails while daring
greatly . . .*

President Theodore Roosevelt
at the Sorbonne in Paris, France
April 23, 1910

Contents

Foreword

Donald M. Berwick, MD, MPP

I am a little embarrassed to admit it, but reading this book made me wish I had an identical twin. As Blair and Fred Sadler—who are identical twins—recount their journey together as a dyad of change agents, bound together by upbringing, values, and love, we witness a deep partnership that is sorely lacking in these fractious, isolating, contentious, modern times. This manuscript uses the words *I, me,* and *my* approximately 270 times. *We, us,* and *our* appear approximately 719 times—more than two-and-a-half times as often. What would the larger world be like with that ratio of commitments?

We need not imagine the answer. These authors don't just preach the embrace of interdependence, they live it. Their account is meticulously generous to others, but Blair and Fred show themselves, over and over, as effective catalysts for structural improvements in healthcare—in organ transplantation policy, in nurturing the identity and roles of advanced practice nurses and physician assistants, in redesigning emergency medical services, and in helping to establish the field of bioethics. They reverse-engineer their effectiveness for the reader in a series of lessons learned, offering guidance for the leadership of change, always emphasizing initiative, optimism, resilience, and above all, cooperation. They know and they show that, with trust and authenticity, people can achieve together milestones that they never, ever could accomplish alone.

Beyond the written lessons, this book also charmingly evinces a brio that must be a root cause of the authors' enormous achievements. How cannot the reader smile when imagining the scene in which twenty-something Blair spots US Supreme Court Chief Justice Earl Warren at a squash match, introduces himself, and ends up, along with Fred, having more than one lunch in Warren's Supreme Court office, teaching him about organ transplantation policy as well as squash? Or reading Blair's account of the seven-hour siege he waged in the waiting room of an associate director at the National Institutes of Health, in order to convince him—successfully—that the NIH should, in an unprecedented move, hire the pair of twins as a single medical-legal team? ("Sometimes," they write, "persistence is not an option. It is the only option.")

Beyond sweetness, there is above all an invaluable example in their unrelenting commitment to help not just others but also each other. At age fourteen, during a fateful tennis match, Blair and Fred made the decision to cooperate rather than compete. They built on that decision year after year after year: in college, in professional training, and in their lifelong shared agendas of progressive public policy. This book leaves no doubt at all that that decision taken in their youth was a keystone to their success throughout their years.

It is no accident that, of all the struggles they have waged together, none seems to grip their imaginations and passions more tightly than their decades-long efforts to improve the policy and management environment for organ transplantation. Perhaps an ultimate form of cooperation—to give of one's own body—organ transplantation reveals the most fundamental values and beliefs we hold about our interdependencies and duties to each other. Blair and Fred's wisdom is evident as they seek the proper balance between absolute volunteerism, which they regard as essential to a proper organ transplantation regime, and a passionate hope to relieve avoidable suffering among the tens of thousands of people awaiting organs.

No matter which of their several quests they describe, Blair and Fred also reveal a level of agility and creativity that marks the best leaders. They always seem to find a pathway out of paralysis and conflict and into shared possibility.

Must one be or have an identical twin to hold and act upon the elements of character that Blair and Fred reveal in this book? These include a commitment to others, total partnership, zest as a team, never accepting *no* as the only answer, never fearing to bring messages to centers of power, and unremitting trust. I hope not. That they share a common genome of course helps these two pioneers team up and render change in the world (and have fun in the process). But in offering us their lessons learned in this gem of a book, they demonstrate that, twins or not, we all have a chance to succeed better together than apart.

I propose that we consider what our world could be like if we all imagined ourselves as twins with each other—if we all imagined that we could feel and act toward each other as Blair and Fred do in this book. How would we then confront a pandemic, roll back climate change, make healthcare a human right, or address racism and poverty? Reading this book gives us a glimpse of what would then be possible. And yes, it makes us a bit envious of the privilege of togetherness that Blair and Fred got by their happy accident of birth.

—Donald M. Berwick, MD, MPP,
President Emeritus and Senior Fellow
Institute for Healthcare Improvement
2022

Preface

(P)LUCK

As a doctor and a lawyer, and identical twin brothers with a history of collaborative teamwork, we decided to write (P)*luck* to share some of the most important lessons we learned along the way. Our hope is to inspire and motivate others who want to make positive changes in the world by using a powerful blend of serendipity and the assertive action required to plunge into unchartered waters.

Pluck is a word often used to describe determination, resolve, audacity, even courage (with the word "luck" built in)—a combination we cultivated. We were fortunate to play key roles in the development of the early laws concerning organ donation and transplantation, the emergence of the brand-new physician assistant profession, the birth of bioethics, and the transformation of emergency medical systems from a wasteland to a vital component of healthcare. Our journey, which began more than fifty years ago, took us inside rooms where major decisions were made that have had a multigenerational impact on healthcare in the United States.

Over a nine-year period, we served as a medical-legal team at the National Institutes of Health, Yale University

School of Medicine, the Robert Wood Johnson Foundation, and The Hastings Center on Bioethics.

The power of collaboration helped us lead and accelerate the pace and scale of critically needed change. In (P) *luck*, we describe the value of a spirit of persistent risk-taking, including taking roads less traveled while embracing a mind-set focused on possibility. Those interested in or committed to making innovations in healthcare, environmental activism; social, economic, and racial equity; or education, will find that significant transformation is possible by drawing on the principles offered in our fifteen lessons for stimulating change.

We invite you to join us on our lived journey of exploration, collaboration, and action.

Introduction

Our First Green Light

Imagine that . . .

*Your father is succumbing to end-stage heart disease, and you
have heard that a heart transplant could save his life. But there
are no laws enabling organ donation, so you have no choice but
to sit by and watch as the man you know and love dissolves into
a husk of himself.*

*A horrifying traffic accident occurs right in front of you. You
rush to the battered cars, eager to assist, and see that the drivers have suffered life-threatening injuries. You want to call for
help, but 911 does not exist. There are no cellphones. When you
finally summon an ambulance, what arrives is a glorified station
wagon, with no medical equipment on board.*

*You work two jobs, but you cannot afford basic healthcare. Your
child's asthma attacks are increasing in severity and frequency.
Finally, a new government program extends health benefits to
your family, but the nearest doctor's office is 50 miles away, and
you must wait four months for an appointment.*

You learn that in 1932, when there were no safe and effective treatments for syphilis, several hundred African-American men were recruited into a study to observe the effects of the disease on them over time. Yet, in the late 1940's, when it was discovered that penicillin could cure syphilis, these men continued to be observed and were never offered the treatment which would have cured them. You realize you live in a country, where that study was supported for decades by the US Public Health Service and the Centers for Disease Control.

Each of these situations sounds like a nightmare. But in 1967, this was healthcare in America. At that time, organ transplantation laws were haphazard and underdeveloped. Medicare and Medicaid had just been enacted to provide health benefits to millions of people, but there were not enough primary care physicians and nurses to serve them. Emergency medical services, where they were available, offered little more than a ride to the nearest hospital. Bioethics—now a staple in medical, law, graduate, and undergraduate schools—did not yet exist as a field of study.

Back then, more than fifty years before starting this book, we worked together as a doctor-lawyer team dedicated to improving healthcare in the United States. During a nine-year period, we learned a great deal about change, and how it can be accelerated to make a difference in peoples' lives.

Our story begins in Philadelphia, where, during our years in medical and law schools, we often considered medical issues through a legal lens, and wondered how an informed perspective on both disciplines could—and perhaps should—impact public policy. We decided to try out some of our ideas in a setting beyond informal discussion. Our first presentation occurred in an amphitheater at Boston's Massachusetts General Hospital. Blair was a newly minted lawyer, and Fred was a medical student in his senior year. Needing to make a presentation as part of his six-week surgical elective, he asked Paul Russell, the attending surgeon, if he could invite Blair to join him in discussing the Good Samaritan question—namely, should doctors stop to render aid at the scene of an accident and risk being sued if the patient didn't do well? Russell enthusiastically agreed.

Though all fifty states and the District of Columbia have Good Samaritan laws, such a policy was relatively new in the mid-1960s.[1] Many debated what form a Good Samaritan law should take. This seemed like an ideal subject for our presentation. We agreed that a sound Good Samaritan policy could benefit society. Certainly, the principle behind it—that people should love and help one another to the best of their abilities—is a foundational teaching, not just of the Christian Bible from which the Good Samaritan parable is drawn, but of every major religion. This talk was an opportunity for us to begin to discover if, how, or where a medical-legal team could pursue interdisciplinary collaboration.

We began our presentation by describing the underlying ethical and legal issues. What were the objectives of a Good Samaritan policy? If the goal was to encourage health professionals and others to help people during medical emergencies, how, in our litigious society, could a helper be protected against a lawsuit in the case of a bad outcome? Clearly the law played a role in balancing the reasonable interests of the victim, while encouraging people to help one another. How should legal immunity be defined, and should it apply only to healthcare professionals or to all people who might stop to lend a hand?

Medical-legal issues had not yet become a broad area of study, but the medical students, interns, and doctors attending our talk had entered their profession because they wanted to help people. They certainly were aware that questions concerning legal liability could cast a shadow over their interactions with patients.

As the Q&A period wrapped up and the audience filed out of the room, Russell told us, "This was one of the best presentations we've had." This was the first of four green lights that were essential for us begin our nine-year collaborative adventure.

We came of age during the reckoning of the civil rights movement, and were called by President John F. Kennedy in his inaugural address to "ask not what your country can do for you—ask what you can do for your country." The late 1960s through the early 1970s were tumultuous years, marked by the Vietnam War and widespread protests, a nationwide coming-to-terms with our country's racist history and policies, the assassinations of Dr. Martin Luther King, Jr. and Robert F. Kennedy, and the resignation of President Richard Nixon.

Beginning in 1967, at age twenty-six, we joined the United States Public Health Service (USPHS) as a medical-legal team, launching a journey that took us from the National Institutes of Health, to The Hastings Center, Yale University Medical School, and ultimately the Robert Wood Johnson Foundation.

We were rookies in the fields of law and medicine when we began our public policy journey, yet we repeatedly found ourselves in the rooms where advances happened; in government agencies, academia, new institutions, and philanthropic foundations.

We witnessed where and how change was accelerated, and we also saw what slowed it. We encountered strategies that opened doors and some that slammed them shut. We met and worked with role models who were effective change agents, and we discovered mentors who selflessly promoted good ideas in the service of common goals. In their inspiring company, we learned to stay open to new opportunities and were impressed by how often doing so seemed to make those opportunities appear.

Our healthcare system and our country will continue to face new challenges, as well as perennial ones. Try to imagine the programs and policies that could be put in place, the resources that could be leveraged, and the personal actions that could be taken—all under the banner of improving health and healthcare *for everyone*. Whether you are volunteering for an hour a week or seeking a direction for your career, if you want to make a positive impact, the possibilities are endless: in healthcare, environmental activism, criminal justice reform, economic inequity, and education reform. Our own experiences described in this book, and the solutions we recommend, demonstrate how transformation is possible, even in a contentious political climate, if we pursue it with courage, creativity, persistence, collaboration wherever possible, and a little bit of pluck.

CHAPTER 1

Taking the Road Less Traveled

Two roads diverged in a wood, and I—
I took the one less traveled by,
And that has made all the difference.

—Robert Frost, "The Road Not Taken"

At our home in Allentown, Pennsylvania, our parents created a culture of intellectual curiosity, espoused tolerance for all people regardless of race or beliefs, and promoted service as a way of life. With a PhD in organic chemistry, our father worked in scientific research throughout his career. He also volunteered as a scoutmaster, promoting service to our community and stewardship of nature. Our mother began her career as an English teacher but also taught mathematics to prisoners at the jail on Rikers Island in New York City. Later she earned a master's degree in psychology and became a counselor.

Our father introduced us to the wonders of nature. Our mother, who sang in choirs and played the piano and organ, immersed us in music and art. They both focused our attention on the world beyond our kitchen table. At a young age, we were reading *The New York Times* on Sundays and having lively family discussions about national and global affairs. Our parents instilled in us a sense of possibility: the drive not only to understand what is, but also to imagine what could be.

We were educated from kindergarten through high school in public schools. Our graduating class at Allentown High had more than 800 students. The school was best known for its champion football, basketball, and wrestling programs. For our undergraduate studies, we were fortunate to receive scholarships to Amherst College, a leading liberal arts college in Massachusetts, recognized for its rigorous academic program and a social environment that mirrored our family's values.

Fred found his medical calling early

When Blair and I were five years old, we both developed severe middle-ear infections. Our mother called our pediatrician, Dr. John Pfromm. Dr. Pfromm appeared in our attic bedroom well past dinnertime on a Friday night, speaking so soothingly that it assuredly was his voice and manner, and not just the tetracycline he gave us, that brought relief.

I wanted to do something that would affect people in the way Dr. Pfromm's visit affected me. During my senior year at Amherst, I accepted a scholarship offer from Hahnemann Medical College (later to become Drexel University College of Medicine) in Philadelphia.

Blair discovered his legal interest in college

My decision to go to law school was conceptual rather than career driven. I didn't necessarily want to be a lawyer, but I saw law school as an opportunity to develop analytical reasoning. Law was great preparation for rigorous thinking and debate. I received a scholarship to attend the University of Pennsylvania Law School.

We graduated from Amherst the year before President John F. Kennedy received an honorary degree from the College and addressed the crowd at the groundbreaking ceremony for the new Robert Frost Library. His speech on October 26, 1963, captured the essence of the school and of that time in our nation:

> [W]hat good is a private college or university unless it is serving a great national purpose? The library being constructed today, this college itself—all of this, of course, was not done merely to give this school's graduates an advantage, an economic advantage, in the life struggle. It does do that. But in return for that, in return for the great opportunity which society gives the graduates of this and related schools, it seems to me incumbent upon this and other schools' graduates to recognize their responsibility to the public interest.
>
> Privilege is here, and with privilege goes responsibility. . . . There is inherited wealth in this country and also inherited poverty. And unless the graduates

of this college and other colleges like it who are given a running start in life—unless they are willing to put back into our society, those talents, the broad sympathy, the understanding, the compassion—unless they are willing to put those qualities back into the service of the Great Republic, then obviously the presuppositions upon which our democracy are based are bound to be fallible.

President Kennedy's remarks amplified a message we heard as students at Amherst, in lectures and seminars, in our advisors' offices, and in our commencement address. The speech he delivered that October day traveled far beyond the Amherst campus, resonating throughout history, not just because it was one of his finer speeches, but also because it was one of his last. He was assassinated twenty-seven days later.

President Kennedy's call to service, combined with the energy of the civil rights movement in the southern states, influenced many young people in our generation to become agents of change. The appeal Kennedy made in that speech still rings true:

The problems which this country now faces are staggering, both at home and abroad. We need the service, in the great sense, of every educated man or woman, to find ten million jobs in the next two-and-a-half years, to govern our relations ... with over 100 countries, to govern those relations with success so that the balance of power remains strong on the side of freedom, to make it possible for Americans of all different races and creeds to live together in harmony, to make it possible for a world to exist in diversity and freedom. All this requires the best of all of us.

Kennedy used Robert Frost's words to beckon the young people of America to take "the road less traveled" in service of the greater good. He understood that taking new paths will often lead to new discoveries, and that our country was in desperate need of them.

What If There Is No Road?

Law school and medical school are known to occupy every waking moment of students' lives, but our busy schedules did not prevent us from getting together. Our schools were just two miles across town. As often as we could, we met up to play tennis or squash or to share a meal with classmates. Just as we had at our childhood kitchen table, or in the dining hall at Amherst, we discussed our latest discoveries, questions, and ideas. With one of us studying medicine and the other law, we found ourselves looking for connections between the two disciplines.

We continued to have these conversations as our graduate and post-graduate education progressed. Blair passed the Pennsylvania bar exam in 1965 and clerked for two appellate judges on the Superior Court of Pennsylvania. He honed his writing skills by drafting judicial opinions and developed a deeper understanding of the judicial system by observing the interactions between the court's seven judges and the lawyers who appeared before them. Fred was finishing his senior year of medical school and preparing to start a surgical internship at the Hospital of the University of Pennsylvania in July 1966.

When we look back, we shouldn't be surprised that we wanted to work together. We had been by each other's sides in many of our biggest endeavors. Collaboration is a hallmark of many twin relationships. So is competition. We remember the moment when we confronted the choice between the two.

We were fourteen years old, slumped on a bench beside a public tennis court, catching our breath, sweat dripping from our faces, our arms hanging like limp dishrags from our shoulders. We had just exhausted ourselves playing a competitive match neither of us wanted to lose. That was when it occurred to us: *What if, instead of struggling against each other in trying to win, we helped each other become better players?*

We became each other's personal hitting partners and coaches. We spent countless hours helping to improve each other's games, which led us to success on the Allentown High School tennis team. In college, we were introduced to squash, developed our skills, and joined the Amherst College squash team, where the same collaborative strategy helped us bring our team to national recognition, ranked fourth in the country. Collaboration had become a core value to us and a lens through which we looked at the world.

The question remained: What could a medical-legal team do in the world, and where could we do this work? To the best of our knowledge, no medical-legal team had pursued a joint career path. We couldn't find any precedent, not even one "less traveled." If we were going to pursue it, we needed to figure out how.

Creating a New Path

During the summer of 1966, we worked together on a position paper that addressed ethical dilemmas that could arise in response to advances in health sciences. We explored areas such as organ donation and transplantation, the use of human beings in research, the Good Samaritan problem, and the evolving definition of death. Writing this paper ignited our curiosity about these issues and helped open our minds to all sorts of options. If we wanted to work on these issues together, how, and where could we do so?

To help us answer these questions, Blair sought the advice of his law school mentor, Prof. Anthony Amsterdam.

Blair reflects

There were countless stories about Anthony Amsterdam's genius, and he lived up to all of them. When I was a student at Penn, someone posted a travel advertisement for the city of Amsterdam on the professor's office door. The ad copy said, "If Amsterdam doesn't amaze you, nothing will." Highly appropriate.

He had a photographic memory that served him so well that he once argued a case before the US Court of Appeals for the District of Columbia with no notes. When he began quoting a case from memory, one of the justices interrupted him and said, "You said that's on page 228? I can't find it."

Amsterdam responded, "I'm sorry, Your Honor, it is on page 228. Your book must be misbound." Indeed, the book was misbound.

Such stories trailed Anthony Amsterdam like gold dust. He had accomplished so much by the time I met him, and he was only in his early thirties. In addition to his achievements as an advocate and a writer, he was an inspiring professor and a generous mentor. When I called and said, "My brother and I have this position paper we've been working on. Would you look at it and tell us what you think?" he didn't hesitate. "Let's meet for dinner," he said.

Fred and I came to the dinner with our paper and two questions. First, did our medical-legal collaboration idea make any sense? Second, could we pursue such a collaboration now, or should we wait until we were further along in our careers?

Amsterdam's eyes were deep-set and intense, and they looked like they could scorch the paper in his hand. When he looked up, his message was clear: "Yes, this is a great idea."

That gave me the courage to ask, "Is it completely absurd to attempt this now?"

"Absolutely not," he answered. "This idea is too good. You should go for it." Then he added, "I have some ideas for your paper," and we preceded to take meticulous notes.

Had Anthony Amsterdam said he was unsure about our idea; we might have halted. Had he said, "Fred, finish your surgical training first," or "Blair, practice law for a few years," we would likely have switched directions. Instead, his reaction switched on a second green light for us. Prof. Amsterdam took us seriously, and that helped us take ourselves seriously. We had a paper to revise and more exploring to do.

In the following weeks, we met after work hours in one of the few air-conditioned rooms we could find: the judge's chambers in City Hall, where the Superior Court of Pennsylvania was housed and where Blair worked.

Fred reflects

Exhausted from grueling shifts at the hospital, I stretched out on the floor of Blair's judge's air-conditioned conference room while Blair clacked away on the typewriter. Temporarily sheltered from Philadelphia's sweltering heat, we worked into the night, honing our position paper.

At the same time, I was getting serious about looking for career opportunities. Although I liked surgery, I was excited by my part in preparing for our Good Samaritan presentation as well as the other times we explored medical-legal issues.

Several of my physician friends were entering the US Public Health Service (USPHS), and I began to inquire about those options. At the National Institutes of Health (NIH), talented young physicians worked in research labs, like those of future Presidential Medal of Freedom winner, Anthony Fauci. Alternatively, doctors could serve at the Centers for Disease Control (CDC) or join the Indian Health Service (IHS), both of which were part of the USPHS. Any of those were viable options, but how could a medical-legal team serve? There was no mechanism for us to apply together. These two-year appointments were designed for individual MDs and PhDs in the medical sciences. They probably wouldn't know what to do with a JD. If we applied to the NIH cold, our applications would likely be ignored. We had to demonstrate the value of a medical-legal collaboration before submitting an application. Who was the right person to read our paper?

Another surgical intern, David Rilling, told me that Luther Terry, who had served as the US surgeon general from 1961 to 1965, had recently become the vice president of health affairs at the University of Pennsylvania's Medical Center. He would know where a medical-legal team could best serve our country. Possibility rang a bell, and it was up to us to respond.

Luther Terry was as known for his bravery as Anthony Amsterdam was for his genius. During his tenure as surgeon general, he took on the tobacco industry, stating boldly and unequivocally in 1964 that smoking was hazardous to your health.[2] He is the reason we have a SURGEON GENERAL WARNING on cigarette packs. Just a year out of his appointment, Terry was now running a major university medical center. He could easily have ignored a request from an intern and a young lawyer to read their fifteen-page paper. He not only read our paper, but he then welcomed us into his office for a discussion.

We didn't need to convince Terry of the relevance of the work we hoped to do. He already knew it was relevant. After having led the nation on health policy issues, he understood the intersection of medicine and law, and he was well-versed in the operations of various health agencies in Washington. He told us, "We've never had a lawyer in the Public Health Service. We should have done this years ago."

Terry still knew many people working at the NIH, and he invited us to use his name and call his successor as surgeon general, William Stewart, as well as James Shannon, the director of the NIH, among others. He also suggested revisions to our paper to help us convince these government leaders that the NIH would benefit from a medical-legal team that would analyze the legal implications of projects they funded, as well as ethical issues they would need to address.

Terry was a true mentor because of his generosity of time, advice, and encouragement. Had fate not placed him at the University of Pennsylvania Medical School, and had he not graciously received two young strangers and their big idea, our path might have ended there. Instead, he flashed our third green light. Encouraged by the reception we received, we applied right away to the USPHS. We drove to Bethesda, where we had numerous interviews in the fall of 1966.

Blair reflects

We received acknowledgments of our applications. Then five months passed with no response. With my judicial clerkship soon ending, I needed to know the direction we were going next. I wasn't sure who to contact at NIH, but I kept remembering how receptive, kind, and caring the associate director, John Sherman, had been during our visit. Maybe he could check on our applications. In February, I drove down to Bethesda, went to NIH, and asked to see him.

Sherman's secretary told me that he had meetings booked all day, but I could wait in the outer office. He might have a few minutes free at the end of the day. I don't think she expected me to do that, but I did. Persistence wasn't an option; it was the only option. I wasn't about to give up now.

When the secretary finally waved me inside, I handed Sherman our paper and reminded him of our visit months earlier. "I remember your visit well," he said. "You have a great idea here, but you haven't heard back from us?" He picked up the phone, and in less than half an hour, our prospects were looking up. He promised to follow up soon. Our fourth green light had turned on. As I drove home that night, possibility shimmered on the horizon once again.

On March 28, 1967, our 26th birthdays, we received Western Union telegrams inviting us to serve in the US Public Health Service, at the rank of senior assistant surgeon, stationed in the NIH director's Office of Program Planning, in Bethesda, Maryland. Through a combination of thorough research, clear writing, collaboration, persistence, serendipity, and generous mentorship, four essential green lights had turned on. We were ready to begin our travels on a new road.

CHAPTER 2

The NIH and Organ Transplantation

Teachers open the door, but you must enter by yourself.

—Chinese Proverb

We met Joseph S. Murtaugh, our new chief at the National Institutes of Health, for the first time on July 3, 1967. He sat behind his desk, looking every bit like Hollywood's image of a 1960's civil servant: white button-down shirt, narrow tie, black-rimmed glasses, and short-cropped hair accented with silver at the temples.

We came to know Murtaugh's brilliance, humility, and unwavering dedication to the American healthcare enterprise. He jokingly called himself one of "the great unwashed" because, unlike his colleagues with an MD or PhD after their names, he did not hold an advanced degree. Still, his genius was no secret. Murtaugh was easily one of the NIH's best writers, and he drafted NIH director James Shannon's annual presentation to Congress, which regularly awarded the NIH more funding than it requested. Whenever the NIH had a public policy or strategic program issue, it usually fell on Murtaugh's desk, as director of the Office of Program Planning.

On day one, we arrived in his office as he was grappling with such an issue, and he wanted to talk to us about it. Stacks of papers were piled everywhere. The phones rang constantly. Murtaugh pushed two newspaper clippings toward us. The headlines were "Bare Human Gland Sale" and "Coroner's Aide Robs Corpses."

"Gentlemen," he said, "we have a problem."

The Pituitary Challenge

Medical advances can often stir up ethical issues, which ripple into two courts: the court of law and the court of public opinion. These news articles described a public relations nightmare brewing at the National Pituitary Agency (NPA), which operated with NIH funding. Founded in 1963, the NPA had been collecting 72,000 cadaver pituitary glands annually for research purposes. The intent was noble.

Scientists at Johns Hopkins University and other academic institutions extracted human growth hormone (HGH) from the pituitary glands, which were used for NIH-funded clinical trials at various centers around the country. Pediatricians and endocrinologists were studying HGH deficiency in children, which affects one out of every 3,800 newborns and causes hypopituitary dwarfism.*

Problems arose in Los Angeles and Minneapolis when some of those glands were taken without consent. When pathology assistants in the local coroners' offices learned that the NPA would pay two dollars (the equivalent of fifteen

---

* In the 1980s, scientists discovered how to synthesize human growth hormone using recombinant DNA technology. In the 1960s however, researchers and patients who needed HGH obtained it from human cadaver pituitary glands.

dollars in 2022) for pituitary glands, they saw an opportunity to make some extra cash. They started taking cadaver glands without obtaining permission from the next of kin and shipping them to the NPA at Johns Hopkins University.

Imagine the public outcry we would hear if people learned that their tax dollars were being used by state medical examiners' offices to fund research on body parts taken and sold without consent. When this story was exposed in the press in the 1960s, the NPA, along with its funder, the NIH, had to deal with the fallout. Joe Murtaugh told us, "I want you to find out everything you can about the law regarding the use of cadaver material for medical purposes and figure out what we need to do to assure our grantees comply."

This was our first assignment as officers in the USPHS. What began as "solving the pituitary problem" led us from the Georgetown Law Library to the Uniform Law Commission, the American Bar Association, Congress, and eventually on a worldwide exploration.

Connectors, Mavens, and Salespeople

Malcolm Gladwell's 2000 book, *The Tipping Point: How Little Things Can Make a Big Difference*, asks why some ideas, trends, and messages take off while others fall flat. Gladwell proposed that trends catch fire when three kinds of people get involved: *connectors*, *mavens*, and *salespeople*. Connectors, as the name suggests, bring people together, intentionally linking individuals in their broad social spheres, for the benefit of both. Mavens accumulate, understand, and share deep knowledge. Salespeople persuade others, in small and large ways, to get on board with new ideas.

Though Gladwell's book was published thirty-seven years after we embarked on our first assignment at the NIH, looking back, we can see the connectors, mavens, and sales-people, in addition to catalytic public events, that pushed forward organ donation law at unprecedented speed.

Our journey to understand the laws relating to the use of cadavers for medical purposes began at the Georgetown Law Library reading tables, where we spent the summer of 1967 poring over legal volumes. We were becoming, accord-ing to Gladwell's terminology, mavens. Back then though, we simply saw ourselves doing what we were trained to do.

Our training in medicine and law taught us that the first step for solving a problem or answering a question was always the same: research. We needed to understand the current body of scientific knowledge and the laws and prec-edents already in the books.

The state laws regulating the treatment of someone's body after death fell into four categories: autopsy statutes, unclaimed body statutes, medical examiner (or coroner) statutes, and, in some states, organ donation laws. If a death occurred due to homicide or suicide, in an accident, or in a case involving a potential threat to public health, such as an infectious disease or viral pandemic, state laws authorized medical examiners to perform an autopsy to investigate the cause, regardless of the next of kin's wishes. These laws, however, did not provide examiners with the legal authority to take cadaver organs or tissues for any other purpose, not even altruistic ones, without consent.

Many states permitted the next of kin to authorize an autopsy on the deceased, but autopsy statutes were not so broad that they authorized the procurement of organs and tissue for donation, education, or research. Several states had laws regarding unclaimed bodies, providing that they could be delivered to medical schools and hospitals for educational purposes, but only after a twenty-four-hour waiting period, during which time the hospital was obliged to seek the next of kin.

Many states had recently adopted organ donation laws, but the statutes varied wildly. Forty-one states had statutes that specifically provided authority to individuals to donate all or parts of their body after their death for medical, scientific, or therapeutic purposes. But these statutes ignored the importance of many medical issues, such as the time sensitivity of organ donation for transplants. Too often, the act of donating was treated as an extension of the distribution of property after death, a process that often took days or weeks, by which time organs were no longer useful for transplantation purposes.

We developed a broader understanding of the laws governing the treatment of dead bodies. Our research helped us discover the nation's leading health law scholars, and we began making calls. We visited health law leaders around the country. In Pennsylvania, we saw Cyril Wecht, who was an MD, JD, pathologist, and the medical examiner for the city of Pittsburgh. We had found his 1966 publication, "The Medico-Legal Autopsy Laws of the Fifty States and the District of Columbia" to be invaluable.[3]

The scope of our research grew beyond the questions, "What are the current laws regarding dead bodies?" and "How do we assure that NIH grantees abide by them?" to "What should organ donation laws be?"

We presented our findings to Murtaugh. The pathology

assistants in California and Minnesota had broken state laws. The NIH needed to take measures to prevent these breaches from occurring again. None of the organ donation statutes in any state provided comprehensive ethical or medically sound guidance for the donation and use of tissue and organs for research or transplantation.

Murtaugh recognized that the NPA's pituitary-gland problems might well apply to any NIH-funded program using cadaver tissue or organs for research. Indeed, several institutes within the NIH were either engaged in or funding research using cadaver tissue or organs. He invited us to present our findings at a weekly meeting, internally referred to as the "College of Cardinals," chaired by NIH director, James Shannon, and attended by the directors of every NIH institute—including the Heart Institute, the Cancer Institute, the Institute of Mental Health, the Institute of Allergy and Infectious Diseases, and the Institute of Arthritis and Metabolic Diseases.

That is how we found ourselves sitting around an enormous mahogany conference table, surrounded by NIH luminaries. We were seventh on the meeting agenda, and when Murtaugh introduced us, he described what had happened with the NPA, what he had asked us to do, and what we had discovered.

"I'm concerned," he told the group. "There could be other places where we are not assuring compliance in programs we fund." He said the institute directors should expect calls from us: "They are going to meet each of you individually. I want you to put them on your calendars, open your doors to them, and show them your lists of grants involving the use of organs and tissue; so they can review regulations, enforcement, and potential vulnerabilities."

Everyone in the room understood the gravity of the situation. Our access to every director at the NIH rapidly expanded our understanding of the breadth of projects the agency funded and introduced us to the major players in the areas of organ and tissue transplantation. That information would prove to be invaluable throughout the coming weeks.

Following Opportunity

As we continued to ask questions and follow up on opportunities, we deepened our expertise and shifted to another "tipping point" role. We became connectors. A month after our "College of Cardinals" meeting, we found ourselves sitting across from Prof. E. Blythe Stason, the mild-mannered former dean of the University of Michigan Law School, who was serving as a commissioner of the Uniform Law Commission (ULC), known then as the National Conference of Commissioners of Uniform State Laws.

The ULC was made up of law professors, lawyers, and judges from each state, whose function was to help make state laws more uniform and current. Since its founding in 1892, the ULC has identified subjects to investigate, then assigned a small working committee to each, charged with analyzing the issues and, if appropriate, developing and drafting a model law for states to adopt. The committees present the model laws to the ULC membership at their annual conference, and the commissioners return to their home states ready to promote the laws to their legislatures.

They traditionally meet one week before the annual meeting of the American Bar Association where their newly adopted model laws are again presented and widely disseminated.

When we met Stason, he was chairing a ULC committee that had been working for a year on a model law related to organ donation and transplantation. Stason's six-member committee had been analyzing the donation issue and developing the first draft of what had been titled the Uniform Gift of Human Tissues Act. Concurrently, we had been examining the existing donation laws, piecing together a nationwide landscape of related research projects, and analyzing how medical research and therapeutics were impacted by donation laws.

Stason fired off questions, and we responded with information, ideas, and questions of our own. He was a law professor in the forty-fifth year of his distinguished career, and he could have shown up as an expert lecturing to neophytes. Instead, he recognized the research we had done and the understanding we had of the medical, legal, and ethical issues involved. He also saw that our work at the NIH had wired us into the medical and scientific communities. He said, "I want you two to be my official consultants on this law."

During this time, Joseph Murtaugh retired from the NIH to become the first staff director of the newly created Board on Medicine of the National Academy of Sciences (later the National Academy of Medicine). Donald Whedon, director of the National Institute of Arthritis and Metabolic Diseases (NIAMD) agreed to supervise us, and we told him about Prof. Stason's invitation to consult on the model law. Whedon immediately understood the importance to the NIH of a uniform donation law and wholeheartedly encouraged our collaboration with the ULC.

At Whedon's invitation, we returned to the weekly NIH directors' meeting to present the findings from our meetings with various institute directors. By the end of that meeting, NIH associate director, John Sherman, directed us to broaden our inquiry into all matters relating to organ donation and transplantation.

Within three months, we had gone from investigating a pituitary procurement crisis to reviewing all NIH grants that used cadaver material, to helping draft a model organ donation law for every state. Along the way, we learned how valuable mentors can be. Murtaugh, Stason, and Whedon entrusted us with great responsibility. They did so because they understood we were all working to solve the same problem, and we had shown them we were up to the task.

Christiaan Barnard Changes Everything

Just five months after we arrived at NIH, an historic event in South Africa brought organ transplantation to worldwide attention. On December 3, 1967, Christiaan Barnard performed the first human heart transplant, at the Groote Schuur Hospital in Cape Town.[4] The procedure sparked a global conversation about transplantation and led *Time* magazine to name Barnard its "Man of the Year."

Transplantation already had a long history, beginning with the first bone graft in 1668, the first skin graft in 1822, the first corneal transplant in 1906, the first cadaveric knee joint transplant in 1908, and the first arterial reconstruction using vein tissue in 1911.[5] Barnard's procedure had also been preceded by kidney, liver, and lung transplants, yet none caused the same stir as the first heart transplant.

Barnard's success generated a flurry of activity in the United States among some high-profile, highly competitive cardiothoracic surgeons, including Adrian Kantrowitz of New York, Norman Shumway at Stanford (under whom Barnard had studied), Michael DeBakey and Denton Cooley in Texas, Thomas Starzl in Denver, and David Hume in Richmond. Unfortunately, the dismal patient survival outcomes after their various heart transplant surgeries revealed that the surgical technique of transplantation was far ahead of immunological science: effective anti-rejection drugs had not yet been developed, and these first transplant patients rejected their new hearts within hours or days. Barnard's first transplant patient, who lived for eighteen days, was considered exceptional.

Public response to these operations ranged from "a miracle" and "the answer to heart disease" to "exceedingly premature," "immoral," and even "criminal." These impassioned reactions seemed tied not only to the heart recipients' bleak outcomes but to the very idea of a heart transplant. An anatomy professor might describe a heart as a "muscular bag," but laypeople saw the heart as much more than its physical function. It was imbued with emotional, aesthetic, and religious meaning.

Organ donation law was a niche subject prior to Barnard's heart transplant surgery, discussed among a small group of scholars. Bioethics and medical law were in their nascent stages of development. After the initial heart transplants though, everyone from experts to the lay public began talking about the subject. Six weeks after the procedure, a Gallup poll proclaimed that seven out of ten people said they would donate their organs to medical science after their death. People also expressed their opinions, critiques, and concerns in newspapers, on television, and on the radio. A cartoon in *The New Yorker* showed a patient in a hospital bed, partially covered by a large sign that said, "Patient asleep—not a heart donor." A bumper sticker cartoon warned, "Drive carefully! Dr. Barnard may be watching."

Heart transplantation raised issues of morality, sociology, philosophy, religion, psychology, economics, politics, and ethics. Congress also took notice. Hearings were held on Capitol Hill under the leadership of democratic senators Walter Mondale and Fred Harris. We were about to learn that, when it came to policy and program development, timing is often the essential ingredient to accelerating change. The need for a new donation and transplantation law for the United States was abundantly clear.

The Uniform Anatomical Gift Act

As we continued our work on the model law, we needed a clear picture of the medical issues relevant to transplantation, such as tissue matching, preserving and transporting organs, evolving surgical techniques, and the new concept of "brain death." We talked with many of the nation's leading researchers in these areas. We met with leaders of agencies and organizations interested in transplantation: the National Kidney Foundation, the Eye Banks Association of America, the American Heart Association, the American College of Cardiology, the American College of Surgeons, the Transplantation Society, tissue banks, and funeral directors' associations.

The model law needed to consider the concerns and needs of these groups while striking a socially acceptable balance that facilitated organ donation and procurement without infringing on deeply held values and rights, particularly those of would-be donors and their families. For instance, how would donors and recipients be selected? How would the law address equity and accessibility? How could the law assure donors that their best interests would be served? How could a law avoid conflict with a person's religious beliefs?

Our research and numerous conversations led us to believe that a successful uniform law needed to balance five interests:

1. An individual's wishes concerning the disposition of his or her body after death,
2. The next of kin's traditional right to possess the deceased's body for burial and religious purposes,
3. Society's need for adequate organs for lifesaving therapy,
4. Society's need for adequate organs and tissue for medical education and research, and
5. Society's need to adequately determine and verify the cause of death in certain circumstances.

What mechanism for organ donation would achieve this balance? Should a model law be based on voluntary consent (sometimes referred to as an "opt-in" principle) by which individuals could choose to become donors? Or should the law include an "opt-out" presumed-consent model, permitting the "routine taking" of organs and tissues unless an individual explicitly objected before death, or unless next of kin objected afterward? Or should the law authorize the compulsory removal of cadaver organs as needed for medical purposes?

Intuitively we stood firmly for voluntary consent as the best option for preserving people's individual rights. Our work on the pituitary problem had shown us the potential damage that "taking of organs or tissue" could do in the court of public opinion. We could imagine the pushback if news broke about a law that allowed the bodies of loved ones to be operated on and organs given away without permission. Not only would this undermine the likelihood of the law being passed, it could undermine the public's attitudes toward organ donation, transplantation, and research.

Prof. Stason agreed. Working closely with him, we developed a completely new draft of what was renamed the Uniform Anatomical Gift Act (UAGA). We avoided unpalatable language, such as references to "harvesting" or "salvaging" organs. As a gift statute, the UAGA was based on consent and would encourage volunteerism. The law's three foundational principles were also cherished American values:

Altruism: The UAGA enabled people to make a gift of life to another human being.

Autonomy: The law preserved an individual's right to decide what happens to his or her body after death.

Trust: The law inspired a patient to trust the medical profession, and the healthcare system, to be fair and to do no harm.

Full Speed Ahead

Blythe Stason and his committee had already been working on a uniform organ-donation law for a full year when we became involved. We were kids compared to everyone else on his team, but we brought many assets they needed: time, access, medical knowledge, and a depth of understanding of the issues. In just six months, we worked together to transform a rough draft into a polished and thoroughly reviewed model law that was approved by the full committee.

Stason could have taken what we offered, integrated it into the law, and sent us home while he carried the completed draft to the ULC's annual meeting. Instead, with the blessing of its executive director, Allison Dunham, he had us present the Uniform Anatomical Gift Act to the more than 100 commissioners—esteemed lawyers, scholars, and judges—from all fifty states. Stason not only opened another door for us, he taught us a fundamental goal of mentorship: create opportunities for the next generation to emerge into leadership roles.

On July 30, 1968, we took our places on the dais in a Philadelphia hotel ballroom in front the commissioners and their staff members. The commissioners seated in the audience were arranged by the state they represented, each showing their state flag. Looking out across the room, it was clear that our model law was facing the scrutiny of leading lawyers from across the nation.

Stason introduced the purpose and principles of the UAGA, then handed the presentation over to us. We described the issues and answered questions. The UAGA was approved by the full body of the conference, without dissent.[6] A model law is just that: a model, until it is introduced into each state legislature. After the meeting, the commissioners had the mandate of returning to their home states to promote the UAGA to legislators who would hopefully vote to adopt it as a state law.

A week later, the ULC took their newly approved model law to the annual meeting of the American Bar Association, also in Philadelphia, where we presented to a much larger audience. It received a strong endorsement. The campaign to promote the UAGA had begun. It now had a tipping point's third necessary ingredient: a team of salespeople, of which we were a part.

Soon we received a flurry of invitations from around the country, asking us to speak about the law. Over the next months, we addressed several state legislatures and testified before the District of Columbia committees of both Houses of Congress. Each of the congressional presentations was memorable, as we spoke in hearing rooms we had seen only on television, answering questions about organ donation and transplantation. Much of our testimony was captured in the Congressional Record.

In addition, our detailed analysis of the thirteen most-important provisions of the UAGA was published in *The Georgetown Law Journal* in October 1968.[7] Our article with Prof. Stason, describing the UAGA, was published in the *Journal of the American Medical Association* in December 1968.[8]

The UAGA had everything necessary to propel it forward: an established apparatus that supported the development of uniform laws; a nationwide network of well-respected commissioners, with Rolodexes full of legislators, to act as its salespeople; a team of mavens available to represent and discuss the law; and a catalytic event that sparked extraordinary national interest and could push legislators to act.

The committee had designed the law to reduce potential opposition and proceed smoothly to adoption. We considered all stakeholders and addressed their needs and concerns. We exercised restraint, recognizing that some organ-donation issues should be addressed by the provinces of medicine, ethics, and other disciplines, while others were better dealt with by the individual states. By design, the UAGA did not legislate issues outside its purview, such as the evolving definition of death. Earlier in 1968, *JAMA* had published a Harvard Medical School committee report describing suggested criteria for brain death.[9]

Confronting a Potential Speed Bump

On August 22, 1968, barely three weeks after the commissioners approved the UAGA, the *New England Journal of Medicine* published "Organ Transplantation: A Proposal for Routine Salvaging of Cadaver Organs,"[10] by UCLA law professor Jesse Dukeminier and physician David Sanders, who promoted a different approach to procuring cadaver organs and tissue. They advocated for "taking" rather than "giving," suggesting that more cadaver material would become available if organs and tissues were routinely "harvested," unless the next of kin explicitly objected. The pair felt there would not be enough voluntary donors to meet the demand.

We saw serious defects in the Dukeminier-Sanders argument. Given that the deceased's family would still need to be asked if they objected to the taking of organs, we believed this approach would not produce more organs for transplantation. We worried about the adverse impact such a thesis, proposed in a highly respected journal, could have, and we needed to refute its views quickly. Fortunately, Sherman and Whedon agreed to write a letter, which the *NEJM* published, calling attention to "numerous errors and omissions" in the Dukeminier-Sanders article and informing the editors that "a detailed response is being prepared which we hope you . . . will consider publishing."

Sometimes a problem is actually an opportunity. Rather than slowing the adoption of the UAGA, the Dukeminier-Sanders article likely helped. It inspired us to write an article with Stason, and Delford Stickel, a Duke University surgeon and colleague who specialized in transplantation, synthesizing our months of conversations with legal scholars, scientists, and medical practitioners. Writing and publishing the article gave us an opportunity to share the finer points of the uniform law with a broad audience.

"Transplantation—a Case for Consent" appeared in the *NEJM* on April 17, 1969.[11] Though the "giving versus taking" debate continued to turn up now and then, nothing slowed the progress of the model law.

With public interest in transplantation soaring, and with solid institutional support in place, the UAGA took off with lightning speed. Of the forty-four state legislatures that met in 1969, forty-one adopted the law as written, including all of its thirteen provisions. By 1971, the model law was adopted in all fifty states and the District of Columbia with no major modifications. In the 128-year history of the ULC, no model law has been adopted as quickly.

CHAPTER 3

Beyond the Uniform Anatomical Gift Act

For it is in giving that we receive . . .

—from the Prayer of St. Francis

The Uniform Anatomical Gift Act supplanted the archaic, cumbersome, and varied donation laws that had preceded it, doing away with one of the major impediments to transplantation. Any person of sound mind, age eighteen (or age twenty-one in a few states), or older, could donate organs and tissues for medical purposes. As the transplantation community learned about the new law, several organizations noted that a gift could be made by any written document, including "a card designed to be carried on the person."

Donor cards had been used by eye banks, tissue banks, and the Kidney Foundation before the UAGA, but their legality had been questioned. The UAGA changed that. To be most effective though, all organizations distributing a donor card needed to use the same one.

UNIFORM DONOR CARD

OF_____
Print or type name of donor

In the hope that I may help others, I hereby make this anatomical gift, if medically acceptable, to take effect upon my death. The words and marks below indicate my desires.

I give: (a) _____ any needed organs or parts
(b)_____ only the following organs or parts

_____
Specify the organ(s) or part(s)

for the purposes of transplantation, therapy, medical research or education;

(c)_____ my body for anatomical study if needed.

Limitations or
special wishes, if any:_____

Signed by the donor and the following two witnesses in the presence of each other:

_____   _____
Signature of Donor   Date of Birth of Donor

_____   _____
Date Signed   City & State

_____   _____
Witness   Witness

This is a legal document under the Uniform Anatomical Gift Act or similar laws.

The uniform Donor Card designed for the donor's wallet

On November 7, 1969, as members of the National Academy of Sciences' Ad Hoc Committee on Medical-Legal Problems, we convened a pivotal meeting of representatives from twenty-one organizations—including the Transplantation Society, Eye Bank Association of America, National Kidney Foundation, National Pituitary Agency, and the tissue bank at the National Naval Medical Center—to develop a donor card that could be used by all.[12] The meeting was a success and produced a simple legal document, the size of a driver's license, that streamlined the consent process and functioned as an educational tool for all organizations involved in transplantation.[13] The uniform donor card is still in use, though computerized donor registries have reduced an individual's need to carry a card.

The Courage to Ask

We worked on the UAGA at the National Institutes of Health, in Bethesda, near the nation's capital. The area was buzzing with energy and filled with people dedicated to fulfilling the promises of democracy. We never knew who we might meet at the NIH cafeteria, on the steps of the Capitol or, on one particular day, at the University Club squash courts, located just a few blocks from the White House, where we were regular players.

Blair recalls

One evening in early 1969, I was watching Fred finish his squash match, waiting for my turn, when I noticed Supreme Court Chief Justice Earl Warren standing a few feet away, also watching the match. It was as if a frog were sitting on each of my shoulders. One said, "This is the perfect time to introduce yourself." The other frog said, "Hell no. He's the chief justice of the United States Supreme Court. Don't bother him."

The first frog won out. I asked, "Mr. Chief Justice, have you ever played squash?"

"No, I haven't," he responded. "Will you tell me the basics?"

We began an easygoing conversation about the rules of the game. "That must be your twin brother down there," he remarked. That turned the conversation to our current project, the UAGA. By this time, Fred had finished his match, and I introduced him to the chief justice. To our amazement, he asked us to visit his chambers to further discuss the UAGA.

A few weeks later, we walked up the steps of the Supreme Court building—excited, nervous, and awed. We expected to be among a large group at this meeting, but a moment later, we were told, "The chief justice will see you now."

We were led into the justice's private dining room and saw a table set for three. We had only a moment to let this information settle before Chief Justice Warren entered. Fortunately for us, he was a genial man who knew how to make people feel welcome. The conversation flowed freely, and he was keenly interested in the complex issues raised by organ donation. As the lunch wrapped up, he requested a copy of our *Georgetown Law Review* article and asked, "Would you like to do this again?" *Would* we? We could hardly believe what had happened—finding the courage to ask a simple question had led to an extraordinary moment.

About a month later, we returned to the chief justice's office. This time, Blair asked him about *Brown v. Board of Education*, the landmark desegregation decision in 1954.

Blair recalls

As a former law clerk to appellate judges in Philadelphia, I understood the sensitive and confidential
dynamics that occurred after the oral arguments in
the cases had been completed, and the judges met
as a group with only their law clerks present. I asked
Chief Justice Warren what had happened in those
chambers in 1954. He was candid in his reply and
said he knew even then that it would be a landmark
case. He felt strongly that the decision should be
unanimous, shared by the court as a whole, and that
he should write it. That is exactly what happened.
A priceless experience in learning with 100% can-
dor his successful strategy to achieve unanimity and
avoid any dissent. Warren achieved his goal with
quiet determination, uncanny instincts, and an in-
tuition that told him when to give and when to hold
firm. I recall drawing on that wisdom in resolving
seemingly intractable disputes.

Going International

Working at the NIH introduced us to people and places we
would never have encountered otherwise, turning us into
frequent fliers and expanding our sense of possibility. Our
roles as mavens and salespeople on behalf of the acceptance
of the UAGA led to invitations to speak at domestic and international conferences in Las Vegas, Houston, North Carolina,
Indiana, Dallas, Montreal, Toronto, London, Paris, Geneva,
Tel Aviv, Athens, and The Hague. Between symposium ac-

tivities, we met with luminaries like pioneering transplant surgeons Norman Shumway, Denton Cooley, and Michael DeBakey; future Supreme Court Justice Lewis Franklin Powell Jr.; and esteemed legal scholar Prof. Paul Freund. We also met with international leaders including Peter Medawar and Roy Calne in England and Jean Hamburger in Paris.

Looking back at the post-UAGA experience, we can see how our willingness to ask questions of others, and request their help, combined with their generosity to foster and further our work. Upon reflection, it's easy to trace how a conversation with a conference attendee during a shared taxi ride, a follow-up letter, an invitation to an association symposium, a handshake at a gala afterward, led to an important contact. Sometimes invitations came to us on their own; other times we had to make the connection.

The Human Impact of Organ Donation

Remarkable bonds are often formed between a donor, their family, and the grateful recipient of a successful organ transplant. Here are three true stories.

Nicholas Green

We often hear stories about the life-changing impact of organ donation on the recipient. But what about the of effects of organ donation on the generous people who, in the face of devastating loss, offer others the gift of life?

In 1994, Californians Reg and Maggie Green traveled to Europe with their children: seven-year-old Nicholas and four-year-old Eleanor. One evening, they were driving on an Italian highway when a car carrying two masked men pulled up alongside them. Mistaking the Greens' car for a jewelry delivery vehicle, one of the men pulled out a gun and shouted for the Greens to pull over. The Greens evaded the robbers, but not before the gunman fired several rounds. One of the bullets hit Nicholas in the head.

For two days, Nicholas lay in an Italian hospital, in a coma. When he was declared brain dead, the Greens responded to their unthinkable tragedy by making the gift of life. Seven recipients received Nicholas's organs. His heart beat for twenty-three more years.

When the Greens' story went public, they received letters of support from all corners of the globe. Italian families still name their children after Nicholas, as have schools and other places in Italy. In the ten years following Nicholas's death, organ donation rates in Italy tripled. No other country achieved such an increase, which has been dubbed "The Nicholas Effect."[14]

Offering the gift of life was Reg and Maggie's only solace in a dark time. They have remained active in efforts to increase organ donation, through The Nicholas Green Foundation.

Nicholas' seven recipients are like many others who need a transplant—a mother who had never seen her baby's face clearly; a diabetic who had been repeatedly in comas; a boy of fifteen, wasting away with a heart disease, who was only the same size as a seven-year-old; a keen sportsman whose vision was gradually darkening; and two children hooked up to dialysis machines several hours a week. Then there was Maria Pia, a vivacious nineteen-year-old girl who the night Nicholas was shot was dying too. Now, against all odds, she's healthy, is married and has two children, one of whom is called Nicholas.[15]

Kenneth Moritsugu

Kenneth Moritsugu, former acting surgeon general of the Public Health Service, had a medical perspective for understanding the importance of organ donation and transplantation. When tragedy struck his family, he understood it personally as well.

In 1992, Moritsugu's wife, Donna Lee Jones Moritsugu, died from injuries sustained in a car accident just a half-mile from their home. She was thirty-seven years old. She left behind her husband and their two girls, Vikki and Erika. Donna's wishes were for the family to make the gift of life. Four people received lifesaving organs, and several more benefited from her corneas and tissues. Through deep sadness, the Moritsugus found empowerment and inspiration in Donna's legacy.

Four years later, tragedy struck the family again, when Vikki was hit by a car on a rain-slicked street. She also died of her injuries. Guided by Vikki's wishes, Moritsugu and Erika made the gift of life once more. Five people received Vikki's organs, and two regained their sight through her corneas.

Moritsugu continues to advocate for donation, urging people to become donors and to communicate their wishes to their family members. He has learned firsthand that organ donation affects more than just donors and recipients. He says, "The circle of life affects them, their families and friends, co-workers and colleagues, and society as well."[16]

Greg Segal

In 2004, Greg Segal received a call no one wants to get. His father, Rick, had collapsed while jogging. At the hospital, Greg learned that a heart transplant could save his father's life, but donor hearts were in short supply.

While Rick waited for a heart, he endured a series of difficult treatments to keep him alive, beginning with life-sustaining drugs and therapies. After three years, Rick's condition had deteriorated, his heart pumping at just 8 percent capacity. Next came a series of high-risk open-heart surgeries to implant two internal devices to help his heart pump properly. With the devices in place, Rick's condition remained tenuous for thirteen months, his lifestyle severely restricted: limited activity, no driving, a strict diet, and two external batteries that needed to recharge every few hours to keep the devices in his chest pumping his heart.

When Rick's situation declined even further, he received 1A recipient status, which moved him up to fifth on the waiting list for thirty days. On the twenty-ninth day, Rick and Greg were called to the hospital because a heart had become available.

The heart had belonged to a twenty-six-year-old IV drug user who died of an overdose, and who might have been HIV positive. If they declined the heart, the likelihood of receiving another before the thirty-day window closed was slim. They decided to go ahead.

Fortunately, the heart was healthy. In 2009, it found a new home in Rick Segal's chest. Eleven years later, he is in excellent health.

For Greg Segal, one family's good fortune was not enough. Medicine had figured out how to transplant a heart, but who was going to untangle the complicated donation system to assure a greater supply of hearts? Greg left his job in venture capital to become an agent of change. With cofounder and international activist Jenna Arnold, he started Organize, a nonprofit patient advocacy organization dedicated to modernizing the organ donation system. Working with the Obama, Trump, and Biden administrations and bipartisan congressional offices, Organize helped to generate new regulations from the US Department of Health and Human Services in 2021. The new "Final Rule" fundamentally transforms how the government evaluates and certifies organ procurement organizations. It also provides congressional oversight on OPO performance.[17]

Organ Donation and Transplantation 1967–1971: Highlights

1967: Alfred and Blair Sadler begin analyzing laws regarding organ and tissue procurement for the National Institutes of Health.

1967: E. Blythe Stason designates the Sadlers as principal consultants to the Uniform Law Commission to help draft a model law.

1967: In South Africa, Christiaan Barnard performs the first heart transplant and is named *Time* magazine's Man of the Year.

1967–1968: Heart transplants are performed in the United States and other countries.

1967–1970: Public interest in transplantation law and ethics skyrockets in response to the first successful heart transplant.

1968: The Uniform Anatomical Gift Act is adopted by the Uniform Law Commission.

1968: The Ad Hoc Harvard Committee on Brain Death publishes its Neurological Criteria of Death.

1968–1971: The UAGA is adopted by all fifty states and the District of Columbia.

1969–1970: A Uniform Organ Donor Card is adopted for use by all organ-donor groups.

CHAPTER 4

The Hastings Center and the Birth of Bioethics

I have a particular trade. I think and write about bioethics, an update and expansion of the ancient field of medical ethics.

—Daniel Callahan, *In Search of the Good: A Life in Bioethics*

Christiaan Barnard's headline-making first human heart transplant catapulted medical ethics to the forefront of public discourse. Around this time, other stunning breakthroughs were occurring in science and medicine, and they were sometimes labeled "the new biology." They included work on end-of-life issues (such as when to terminate active medical interventions on a hopelessly ill and dying patient), genetic screening and engineering, and new definitions of death. All of them raised ethical dilemmas and debates, but at the time no organization or institute actively addressed the ethical issues posed by these advances.

In late 1968, two leading activists began discussing their insights that advances in biomedical technologies, like ventilators and dialysis, were having a profound impact on society, with the potential for great benefit but also significant harms, if not managed mindfully. Daniel Callahan, trained as a philosopher, was also a former editor of *Commonweal* magazine, a respected American Catholic journal of opinion. Willard Gaylin was an esteemed New York psychoanalyst and a clinical professor of psychiatry at Columbia University Medical School, where he had studied and interviewed young men who chose to go to prison rather than fight in what they considered to be the grossly unethical war in Vietnam. They realized there was no institution dedicated to studying the social and ethical impacts of emerging life sciences knowledge and biomedical innovation.

They discovered that they each thought deeply about ethical issues. As their conversations continued, Callahan and Gaylin discussed establishing an institute to study a broad array of ethical issues. This was the beginning of the process that would lead to The Hastings Center.

We were not aware of what Callahan and Gaylin were planning, but we read a *Washington Post* opinion piece about organ transplantation by Leon Kass, a physician acquaintance of ours at the NIH, that brought us into Hastings's beginnings. During a lunch, Kass enthusiastically described some recent discussions he had attended, hosted by Callahan and Gaylin. He suggested we join him for one such meeting. A few weeks later, in early 1969, we were on a train together to New York.

In the following weeks, enthusiasm grew for creating a new, independent, center on bioethics – one that would combine the rigor of academic scholarship with a commitment to plain language accessible to the public, reflecting

Callahan's years of experience as a journalist as well as a philosopher. Callahan and Gaylin lived in Hastings-on-Hudson, outside New York City, and the headquarters for the center would be located there. The Hastings Center (originally called the Institute for Society, Ethics, and the Life Sciences) was formally incorporated in August 1969. A core principle was that it would be freestanding, which would allow it to collaborate with multiple organizations throughout the United States and internationally.

The personal chemistry of Callahan and Gaylin was remarkable. Gaylin was outgoing, with high energy and a resonant voice, while Callahan was softer spoken, cerebral, and reflective. They established a culture of inclusiveness, generosity, courage, and sensitivity that continues. As co-leaders of The Hastings Center, they made a great team.

Despite our lack of formal training in ethics, they recognized our experience with the ethical issues surrounding organ donation and transplantation, and invited us to participate in the Hastings conversations.

As the 1970s progressed, Congress was highly supportive of biomedical research. NIH budgets were increased significantly each year. Much of the research involved human subjects, many of whom served as "volunteers." The NIH had already begun to address issues around the type of information that patients should receive about the risks and benefits of the procedures they were taking part in.

In 1966, Henry Beecher had published an important article in the *New England Journal of Medicine,* warning that scientific developments can have a human cost. The article provided twenty-two examples of unethical or questionably ethical scientific studies conducted on human subjects at "leading medical schools, university hospitals, private hospitals, governmental military departments (the Army, the Navy and the Air Force), governmental agencies (the National Institutes of Health), Veterans Administration hospitals, and industry."[18]

The article raised troubling questions about how society balances the competing values of scientific progress and individual rights. In 1972, a report surfaced about the infamous Tuskegee syphilis experiments. Beginning in 1932, when there were no safe and effective treatments for the disease, hundreds of African American men were recruited into a longitudinal, observational study to document the natural history of the disease. In the 1940s while the study was still going on, it was discovered that penicillin could cure syphilis, yet no one offered the medication to the men in the study, which continued for decades more with support from the Public Health Service and the Centers for Disease Control. This failure to provide life-saving treatment was uncovered by Peter Buxtun, an epidemiologist working for the NIH, and brought to public attention by an investigative journalist, Jean Heller.[19]

These were the kinds of vitally important ethical issues that The Hastings Center would address. Hastings and its scholars-in-residence wrote articles and books and led discussions on ethical issues in health, science, and technology that informed policy, practice, and public understanding of bioethics. In addition to full-time scholars based at Hastings, the center established a network of Fellows who were located elsewhere but who actively participated in the center's work. We were invited to become Founding Fellows of The Hastings Center.

In its earliest days, the center hosted conversations with Fellows like Paul Ramsey, Hans Jonas, and William May, all of whom had taken an interest in ethical issues surrounding organ donation. As policymakers, we were eager to hear how the recently approved UAGA measured against these ethicists' perspectives.

Ramsey, a professor of Christian ethics at Princeton University, powerfully articulated a preference for the voluntary donation of organs over the "routine salvage" approach. He concluded: "A society will be a better human community in which giving and receiving is the rule, not taking for the sake of good to come." He said that by "answering the need for gifts by encouraging real givers," the consent approach "meets the measure of authentic community among men."[20]

Jonas, a professor of philosophy at New York's New School for Social Research, addressed the critical need for public confidence in physicians relating to respect for life. "The patient must be absolutely sure that his doctor does not become his executioner," he warned, "and that no definition (of death) ever authorizes him to become one."[21] A major reason we opted not to include a definition of death in the UAGA was that the concept was new, controversial, would most certainly evolve, and might complicate adoption of the law. Like Jonas, we believed any organ donation policy must foster and protect trust between patient and physician.

May, a professor of moral theology at the Catholic University of America in Washington, DC, observed, "While the procedure of routine salvaging may, in the short run, furnish more organs for transplants, in the long run, its systemic effect on the institutions of medical care would seem to be depressing and corrosive of that trust upon which acts of healing depend."[22] We also were informed by the ground-breaking sociological work of Renée Fox and Judith Swazey, which focused on transplant patients and donor families.[23]

Our regular discussions with bioethics leaders at Hastings further reinforced our convictions about the importance of protecting the underlying values of voluntary donation and consent in the UAGA. We published our analysis of legal alternatives to providing cadaver organs for transplantation in the inaugural issue of *Hastings Center Studies,* the original title of the center's flagship journal, now known as *The Hastings Center Report.*[24]

The center also created multidisciplinary task forces that addressed particular issues, such as brain death. We participated in the Death and Dying Taskforce, a twenty-four-member group that studied the scientific and ethical issues related to the scientific criteria for brain death. The findings were published in 1972 in the *Journal of the American Medicine Association.*[25]

Over time, we have found that the groundbreaking work carried out by The Hastings Center has provided important perspectives on a wide array of questions our society must tackle, including ethical issues in genomics, in neuroscience, in a vast array of health and science policy questions, in public health ethics, clinical ethics and research ethics.[26]

CHAPTER 5

The Healthcare Workforce Crisis

Start where you are. Use what you have. Do what you can.

—Arthur Ashe

As our two-year commitment at the NIH drew to a close, we wondered how we could continue our partnership. Our time in Washington had changed us profoundly, and we could not imagine returning to practicing law at a firm or resuming a surgical residency. The creation and the success of the UAGA had shown us that significant change could be achieved in a short period of time. We wanted to continue our medical-legal collaboration.

Our next project picked us. In the spring of 1969, we were called by Dr. Roger Egeberg, assistant secretary for health in the Department of Health, Education, and Welfare (HEW). The department was putting together a team to find solutions to the massive shortage of healthcare professionals in the United States. To join the team, we signed on for a third year as commissioned officers in the Public Health Service. In addition to this work, Fred was managing the urology and renal disease grant program at the Institute of Arthritis and Metabolic Diseases under Donald Whedon, and Blair was working under Kenneth Endicott, director of the Cancer Institute, actively informing states about the UAGA and related issues.

Several visionaries had begun piloting training programs for new categories of healthcare personnel to practice general medicine without the requisite seven-plus years of education and training required of a physician. Three of these pioneering programs (at Duke University, the University of Colorado, and the University of Washington) were being funded by private foundations, and they caught the attention of Egeberg and others at HEW. They wanted to know more about what these educators were doing, whether they offered a viable solution to the workforce shortage, and whether HEW should use federal funds to support such programs. Among their questions about these new programs was whether they could thrive at other medical schools. And if so, how could those newly minted primary care providers be licensed?

Before undertaking these visits, we needed to take a deep dive into the health manpower field and understand the key issues.

The Healthcare Shortage

Two developments converged in the 1960s to exacerbate a serious health manpower shortage in the United States.

First, on July 30, 1965, President Lyndon B. Johnson signed into law the bill that created Medicare (for people sixty-five and older) and Medicaid (for people below a defined income level) to fund much-needed healthcare to tens of millions of Americans. Unfortunately, the country did not have nearly enough health professionals to provide the necessary healthcare.

Second, the rapid progress in medical science and the invention of new technologies had led to the growth of medical and surgical specialties, such as pulmonology and cardiology. As a result, most medical students were bypassing the "general practitioner" path in pursuit of becoming specialists and subspecialists, thus siphoning off much of the needed supply of general medicine doctors while keeping doctors in training longer.[†]

Experts in what we then called "health manpower" began debating how to increase the number of health practitioners and deploy them to the locations that needed them most, particularly rural and underserved urban areas. The National Health Service Corps was created, and private foundations like the Carnegie Corporation, The Commonwealth Fund, the Foundation for Child Development, the Josiah Macy Jr. Foundation, and The Rockefeller Foundation also invested in health workforce expansion programs. Federal agencies investigated a range of solutions, including expanding the size and number of medical schools, and funding education for physicians. The problem was time. Seven or eight years would go by before newly recruited

---

† Traditionally, a doctor's education included four years of medical school, after which graduates enrolled in a twelve-month internship. Typically, these were rotating internships, during which interns spent time learning general medicine, surgery, obstetrics/gynecology, pediatrics, and psychiatry. After those rotations, and after passing certifying examinations, the new physician was credentialed to practice general medicine. Medical students wishing to pursue a specialization enrolled in advanced training residencies, which lasted three to five more years, and culminated in a qualifying specialty exam. Subspecialties, such as cardiology and pulmonology, soon followed, which meant an additional two-year fellowship. Add it all up, and a future cardiologist or pulmonologist could be in medical school for four years, then in training for five more.

medical students completed their long training to became practicing doctors.

Medical Care without Medical School

The idea of a nondoctor offering a doctor's services brings up all kinds of images, from a huckster selling elixirs out of the trunk of his car to a charlatan on trial for practicing medicine without a license. But the history of medical care also includes many examples of highly skilled nonphysicians who provided excellent and essential health services.

Mary Breckinridge is an inspiring example. A southerner by birth and a nurse by training, Breckinridge joined the American Committee for Devastated France in 1919, serving people in post-World War I French villages. At home, she believed the nurse-midwifery model she encountered during the war could solve many of the health problems she had witnessed in the American rural south. She established the Kentucky Committee for Mothers and Babies, later known as the Frontier Nursing Services (FNS), the first US organization of nurses trained as midwives providing care under the direction of a medical doctor.

The FNS nurses, Breckinridge included, often traveled by horseback to reach their patients. Within four years, FNS had opened a rural outpost clinic and staffed a hospital. Eventually they established a Graduate School of Midwifery, now Frontier Nursing University. FNS nurses proved that properly trained nonphysicians could bring high-quality health care into underserved areas. In their first thirty years of operation, they had better maternal and infant outcome statistics than the country as a whole,[‡] even though their services were provided in remote areas that were often unreachable by automobiles.

Some forward-thinking doctors also began training trusted assistants. Among the most famous of these assistants was Vivien Thomas. Born in 1910, the grandson of a slave, Thomas was in his first year of medical school when the banks crashed in 1929, wiping out his earnings and forcing him to leave school. Soon after, Thomas landed a job at Vanderbilt University as a laboratory assistant for Alfred Blalock, and he set out to learn all he could, quickly mastering research methods and surgical techniques. Thomas became an integral part of Blalock's surgical team, although—in a stinging reminder of the racism of that time—he was classified and compensated as a janitor. When Johns Hopkins University recruited Blalock, he insisted that he and Thomas were a team. At Johns Hopkins, Thomas and Blalock broke new ground in surgical technique.[27]

Blalock was approached by renowned pediatric cardiologist, Helen Taussig, who hoped to find a surgical solution to a complex and fatal heart anomaly called the Tetralogy of Fallot, also known as "blue baby syndrome." Thomas was given the assignment of creating a blue baby-like condition in a dog, then correcting it surgically. After nearly two years of work involving some 200 dogs, Thomas demonstrated that the corrective surgical procedure functioned and was

---

‡ In 1933, Metropolitan Life Insurance Company published a summary of data from 1,000 Frontier Nursing Services births, concluding "the services provided by FNS significantly decrease maternal and neonatal mortality." By 1954, FNS had overseen 10,000 births. See https://frontier.edu/about-frontier/history-of-fnu/.

safe, persuading Blalock that the operation could be attempted on a human patient.

During that first procedure, performed on baby Eileen Saxon in 1944, "Blalock insisted Thomas stand at his elbow, on a step stool where he could see what Blalock was doing. Thomas had done the procedure dozens of times; Blalock only once, as Vivien's assistant." Denton Cooley, present as a medical student that day, recalls "the tension in the operating room . . . as Blalock rebuilt a little girl's tiny, twisted heart, . . . how that baby went from blue to pink the minute Blalock removed the clamps and her arteries began to function," and "where Thomas stood—on a little step stool, looking over Blalock's right shoulder, answering questions and coaching every move."[28]

In 1976, Thomas, who never went to medical school, eventually received an honorary doctorate degree from Johns Hopkins, and officially joined the medical school faculty there. He helped train some of our country's finest surgeons, Cooley among them.

The Blalock-Thomas team accomplished exceptional work, but their arrangement, a doctor delegating medical tasks to a nonphysician, was not uncommon. Many physician educators and practicing physicians had served in the Korean or Vietnam wars. They had witnessed military corpsmen, with eighteen months of intensive training at US military medical centers, responding to battlefield trauma and stabilizing the wounded until they could be transported to a base hospital. They were truly lifesavers under the most difficult circumstances.

Medical schools that had voluntarily sent teams of physicians and surgeons to staff mobile military hospitals, like the one featured in the 1970's television show *M*A*S*H*, understood how corpsmen were essential to the medical team and recognized the potential for adapting the same model back home. A logical next step was for medical schools and federal agencies to look to these nonphysicians to help solve the doctor shortage. Given the situation's urgency, it was time to explore new solutions.

Begin Again

As we began our new assignment, we felt enthusiastic and energized. We didn't know much about health manpower issues, though we had learned a few things about becoming mavens. We took up residency in the National Library of Medicine, located adjacent to the NIH campus, where we immersed ourselves in current health manpower data, projections, and theories. We read the articles and contacted the authors. Thanks to our HEW credentials, they answered our calls, and because we were all working toward the same goal, resolving the healthcare manpower crisis, they connected us to the next person in the chain of people we needed to meet.

Our path led us to Thomas Hatch, who oversaw funding of allied health manpower programs at HEW, and to Douglas Fenderson, who was a leading strategist in addressing health manpower shortage problems and solutions at NIH's Bureau of Health Manpower Education. Their perspectives and advice were invaluable in understanding the big picture. We were now ready to visit the pioneers that Egeberg had identified.

Eugene Stead and Thelma Ingles, Duke University

Eugene Stead was one of the country's most-prominent professors of medicine. In his efforts to expand our country's healthcare capacity, he focused first on existing care providers, particularly nurses. He asked, "Why aren't nurses trained to take on a larger role in healthcare?" In 1958, he partnered with Thelma Ingles to address that question.

Ingles, an outstanding nurse educator, was chair of medical-surgical nursing at the Duke University Nursing School. She was highly intelligent, well trained, and looking for a new direction. Stead suggested that he and his physician colleagues train her during her sabbatical year to do much of what a doctor does, enabling her to function at an entirely different clinical level. If the training worked for Ingles, Stead speculated, they could set up a training program for other nurses as well.

At the end of her year-long training, Ingles and Stead had developed a curriculum for the nursing school, formalizing a masters-level, one-year intensive training program in advanced clinical care. Ingles recruited the best and brightest nurses for the prototype program, which those nurses completed the following year.

Stead and Ingles sought accreditation for Duke's advanced nursing program from nursing's accrediting body, the National League for Nursing (NLN). However, the NLN representatives refused to accredit the program, saying it had so much doctor input, it was no longer a "nursing program." They were also bothered that Ingles, the program director, did not have a baccalaureate degree in nursing (she had completed a rigorous, three-year registered nurse diploma program at the Massachusetts General Hospital, but her bachelor's degree was in English from UCLA). Stead and Ingles tried for accreditation a second time, only to be rebuffed again.

Stead and Ingles wanted to provide nurses with advanced patient-care training, but the accrediting body, the NLN, wouldn't allow it. Stead decided it was fruitless to work with an organization that refused a golden opportunity for nurses and for healthcare in general, all because of its parochial, anti-physician stance.[29] Thelma Ingles moved on to The Rockefeller Foundation, where she had a remarkable career working in fifty-five countries to establish innovative programs for underserved populations.[30]

Stead did not let the NLN decision stop him. Amos Johnson, a highly respected general practitioner from Garland, North Carolina, often attended the continuing education classes Stead had been offering for practicing physicians. During a conversation with Johnson, Stead asked how he managed to leave his practice regularly. The answer was Buddy Treadwell.[31]

In 1940, Johnson had hired and trained a young African American man named Henry Lee "Buddy" Treadwell to be his "doctor's assistant." As Treadwell's knowledge and skills developed, and Johnson became involved in more medical organizations, he increasingly was able to leave his general practice in Treadwell's capable hands. Treadwell was so well accepted by patients that they were comfortable with his decision-making and care, knowing that he would contact Johnson if a situation required more than he could handle. In some cases, Johnson gave Treadwell directions over the phone, and other times Treadwell sent the patient to another doctor or directly to the hospital. The Buddy Treadwell story reinforced Stead's belief that properly trained nonphysicians could offer high-level healthcare.

Stead also knew that as the Vietnam War was expanding, thirty thousand corpsmen who had tended to the wounded on the battlefield, helped to stop bleeding, started IVs, splinted fractures, and assisted in the triage areas and ORs in base-camp hospitals, were being discharged from the military every year. In a degree-oriented, civilian healthcare system, when they knocked on hospital doors, looking for work, they would not be asked "What can you do?" Rather, they were asked, "Where did you go to medical school?" or "What kind of degree do you have?" Some would be hired as orderlies, if at all, and paid a minimum wage. Stead had the foresight to look beyond the degree to the person's actual experiences and acquired skills, and to recognize that these men and women represented a large pool available for civilian training programs to help provide medical care.

Several former corpsmen had landed medical jobs at Duke. In 1965, Stead invited four of them to join the inaugural class of what he called the physician's assistant (PA) program. He proposed to build on their training and experience by putting them through a mini-medical school experience, where twenty-four months of intensive coursework and clinical training prepared them for useful patient care functions.

Stead's program immersed students in core material: basic anatomy, physiology, and other essential disciplines, followed by studies of injury, disease, and pharmacology. Next they worked under an internist, pediatrician, or surgeon, much as medical students and residents did. After two years, the student was certified by the Duke University School of Medicine as a physician's assistant (PA). The competency-based, generalist curriculum prepared graduates to work with a primary care doctor or to assist a surgeon if they were interested in specializing. In either case, the doctor and the new PA would work out the scope of their joint practice.[32]

Three of the four men who joined Duke's first PA class graduated on October 6, 1967. By the time we visited the Duke program in 1969, Stead was no longer wondering why nurses weren't doing more. He was trying to figure out how his outstanding PAs could become certified and licensed to work in healthcare settings.

Henry Silver and Loretta Ford, University of Colorado

Pediatricians at the University of Colorado Medical School who wanted to provide healthcare to underserved populations donated their time, usually a half-day a week, to public health clinics in the area. As helpful as this was, it didn't come close to meeting the demand for care. In 1965, two pioneers decided to act: Henry Silver, one of the country's most respected pediatrics professors, and Loretta Ford, a visionary nurse and educator in the School of Nursing's public health department.

Silver and Ford observed that nurses were limited to doing vaccinations and well-baby checks. They believed nurses could do much more. They invited nurses to enroll in a four-month training course, followed by an eight-month clerkship, working under the direction of pediatricians in the community. The nurses received no degree after the year of training, but they were certified as pediatric nurse practitioners (PNPs).[33]

Silver was impressed by the PNPs' success, furthering his belief that nonphysicians could take on tasks previously performed only by doctors. He knew about Stead's experience with the NLN, and he didn't want to deal with organized nursing and its credentialing restrictions. Like Stead, Silver pursued the physician assistant route, focusing on pediatrics. The Child Health Associate (CHA) program was officially launched at the University of Colorado in 1969.[34]

Ford was having her own struggles with the nursing school dean, who looked skeptically at the PNPs. The dean saw the expansion of clinical nursing services as a threat to nursing tradition and offered no encouragement for this evolution.

Silver designed the CHA program not only for people with prior medical experience, but also for those with two to three years of college. After the two-year program, graduates earned a baccalaureate degree. Then after an intensive, one-year internship in pediatrics, they were awarded a master's degree. To support Silver's proposition that the CHA graduates offered a viable solution to the workforce shortage, he and his colleagues diligently documented the competence, efficiency, and effectiveness of each practicing child health associate. Silver was very highly regarded, and with the active support of Dean Richard Krugman, they were able to persuade the state legislature to pass a new law that enabled CHAs to "practice pediatrics."

In 1972, Ford accepted an outstanding offer from the University of Rochester Medical Center to establish a new school of nursing as its founding dean and chief of the nursing services at Strong Memorial Hospital in Rochester, New York. She spent her professional career advocating for and enhancing advanced nursing roles in collaboration with physicians. She celebrated her 101st birthday on December 28, 2021 and remains active in the field as of this writing.

Richard Smith, University of Washington

By the time Richard Smith arrived at the University of Washington in 1967, he had already worked with the Peace Corps in Nigeria, served as director of field operations for the Office of Equal Opportunity, and helped to desegregate numerous hospitals after the passage of the Civil Rights Act and Medicare. In the Office of the Surgeon General, as director of International Health Manpower Planning, he was, in 1967, the youngest and the first Black person appointed to the US delegation for the World Health Assembly in Geneva. These experiences, along with his charismatic personality, made Smith an international healthcare leader and shaped his vision for a new category of healthcare practitioner.

In 1969, at the University of Washington, he founded the first MEDEX (Medical Extension) program to extend the healing hands of overburdened physicians into rural areas of eastern Washington, where the population was so sparse it couldn't sustain regular medical services. Smith determined that having nondoctors provide much of the care along with physicians was the only way to get healthcare to those rural areas.

Smith created his MEDEX program in collaboration with the University's School of Medicine, the Washington

State Medical Association, primary care doctors, and community members. When MEDEX began, the entire curriculum lasted fifteen months, with three months of academic learning at the university and one year of clinical training with a family practice doctor. This model appealed to students who couldn't afford the many years of medical school and who wanted to get started in medical practice. Smith also drew upon former military corpsmen for his students.[35]

The MEDEX program encouraged established general practice doctors, many of whom were overextended and burned out, to take on students: professional helpers that these doctors could personally train and eventually hire. Once a MEDEX student was paired with a doctor, the student shared the doctor's patient load while also learning all the doctor had to teach. Being trained by a single doctor, however, could be limiting for students, who benefit from having more than one teacher. Eventually, the MEDEX program's fifteen-month curriculum was extended to twenty-four months, and the model of working under only one doctor changed as well. During our visit with Smith in 1969, we saw that his MEDEX students were already making a difference in the rural communities outside Seattle.

Smith, like Stead at Duke and Silver at Colorado, envisioned MEDEX as a pilot program with great potential to help solve the doctor shortage. These visionary leaders wanted their programs to grow far beyond their own universities, graduating thousands of new medical professionals to serve people in the farthest reaches of the country. For that to happen, they needed a legal way for their graduates to practice medicine.

A recent, rapid expansion of new kinds of healthcare

professionals, such as respiratory therapists, radiology technicians, and laboratory technicians, many funded by HEW, were important advancements because they each took on tasks previously performed by doctors, freeing them to see more patients. But the process of licensing these professionals had become convoluted, duplicative, and sometimes divisive. Several academic studies concluded that licensing wasn't effectively protecting the public from the occasional unscrupulous practitioner. The American Medical Association, American Hospital Association, and HEW stated that until that process was improved, they supported a moratorium on licensing for new categories of healthcare professionals. This included the new physician assistant profession, a major hurdle we faced when it was time to recommend a new licensing law.

The pioneers of the PA, CHA, and MEDEX programs couldn't wait years for the licensure issues to be resolved. Nor could Egeberg. The country needed new health practitioners now. The graduates of these programs could multiply rapidly, but without licensing they would have trouble being employed.

We headed back to the Georgetown Law Library. This time, we reviewed the fifty states' laws on nonphysician health practitioners. Some states licensed twelve different healthcare professions, while others had as many as twenty-six. All had some form of a medical practice act that regulated physician practice in that state.

We knew our way around the Uniform Law Commission, and a uniform model law could be a natural solution for this problem. But creating a uniform law would take three years or more, time we didn't have.

Fortunately, we weren't the only ones looking at the states' medical practice acts. During our visit to Duke University, we met with Harvey Estes and Martha Ballenger. Estes chaired the newly formed Family and Community Medicine Department, which housed the PA program. Ballenger was a talented lawyer. They were researching various perspectives on the law for PAs to be licensed.[36] They shared their ideas, concerns, questions, and challenges. Our collaboration led us all to agree that the simplest approach was to amend each state's medical practice act.

The medical practice act defined the legal practice of medicine, typically with four words: operate, diagnose, treat, and prescribe. Only a physician could perform these functions, though some nonphysicians could perform some of them to a limited extent, under a physician's supervision.[37] Nursing practice acts stated that nurses could evaluate, observe, and make a nursing diagnosis, but they could not make a medical diagnosis.

We decided that adding a single sentence to each state's medical practice act could open the door for new, properly trained medical professionals to practice medicine. The sentence read:

Nothing in the above language shall prevent a physician from delegating to a specially trained nurse, nurse assistant, or physician's assistant those tasks that the assistant is qualified to carry out, and as long as that task is carried out under the supervision, control, and responsibility of a licensed physician.[38]

Some fifty years later, a leading PA health policy expert, David Keahey, likened this solution to Occam's Razor. This principle, attributed to thirteenth-century Franciscan friar, William of Ockham, is frequently used in scientific circles when discussing competing theoretical options. It states that, of many possible answers that can account for all facts, the simplest answer is often the best.[39]

The report we wrote about our discoveries during the health manpower project came to a little more than 100 pages. We presented our findings to Kenneth Endicott, who had recently moved from directing the Cancer Institute to become director of the Bureau of Health Manpower. He endorsed our report and its recommendations and delivered them to Egeberg at HEW.

Once our research was complete, it was time for each state to amend its medical practice act. We knew many leaders in medicine and law (including Malcolm Todd, the president of the AMA) and we joined our Duke colleagues, acting as connectors, conferring with the proper stakeholders, and rallying the right salespeople to tip the states' legislatures in favor of physician assistants as newly credentialed health professionals. By 1973, within just three years, the majority of states had amended their medical practice acts to allow physician's assistants to work in collaboration with and under the supervision of physicians.[40]

CHAPTER 6

Crafting a New Profession: The Physician Assistant

I dwell in Possibility—
A fairer House than Prose—
More numerous of Windows—
Superior—for Doors—

—Emily Dickinson, "I dwell in Possibility"

Our work on health workforce solutions was very encouraging. We believed that the right deployment of new healthcare programs and professionals, like the physician assistant (as the profession has come to be known), MEDEX, and the child health associate, could mean fewer long waits in emergency departments, shorter waits to see a physician, and an expanded, highly skilled healthcare workforce. Exciting as this was, our time at the NIH was about to end, and we needed to figure how best to continue our work together.

Fred recalls

During our third year with the Public Health Service, while I also managed the renal disease grant program for the National Institute of Arthritis and Metabolic Disease, I visited universities that applied for or had received grants from NIH. I was scheduled to meet with the Yale department of physiology, and decided to visit my favorite medical school professor, who was now chair of the department of surgery at Yale Medical School.

Dr. Jack Cole exuded the caring manner of the pediatrician who had cared for Blair and me and who had inspired me to go into medicine in the first place. Those same qualities in Cole had spurred me to pursue a career in surgery.

I hadn't seen him in three years, but he put me at ease immediately. On his desk was the 1969 article Blair and I had written for the New England Journal of Medicine about transplantation. He nodded at it and said, "I've been following you lads and the wonderful work you have been doing."

That's when the meeting turned from reunion to job interview. "I've recently obtained a two-million-dollar grant from The Commonwealth Fund of New York to study trauma and emergency medicine," Cole explained. "I want Yale's department of surgery to do something about our country's woeful state of emergency care. We do quite well in this hospital once the patient gets to our operating theater. The question is whether they can get here alive, because the out-of-hospital system is in dire need of upgrading."

Cole wanted to establish a trauma program at Yale to study the state of emergency care outside the hospital. He wanted to be able to identify areas for improvement and to implement solutions in every area of emergency medical service: from ambulances and communication systems, to training for healthcare professionals, from first responders to emergency room physicians and nurses.

"I've interviewed a number of senior surgeons and retired professors," he said, "but I think you two would be a great team to run this. You would direct the trauma program out of the department of surgery. Would this interest you?"

I understood from our conversation that Cole would let us take the same approach we had taken with transplantation and health manpower: study the problem, connect with stakeholders, identify key issues, and collaborate to create solutions. That was the moment when I first thought that emergency medical services might be our next project.

"I know we would be interested," I responded. "Let me talk with Blair about it." I was truly excited about this opportunity: working with Jack Cole, at Yale University, with a two- million-dollar budget— the equivalent of fourteen million dollars in 2022. I could not wait to talk to Blair.

Emergency medical services desperately needed a complete overhaul, and we agreed that directing the Yale Trauma Program seemed ideal. We weren't ready to give up our passion for PA-type programs though. When we proposed a physician assistant program under the umbrella of the trauma program, Dr. Cole immediately saw the connection and wholeheartedly agreed.

We joined the Yale Medical School faculty on July 1, 1970, to conduct a comprehensive study of emergency medical services, using the state of Connecticut as a test case. We were also going to launch a robust physician assistant program that would broadly train practitioners to assist in emergency and general medicine. Fred was appointed an assistant professor of surgery and public health, and Blair was an assistant professor of law.

Riding the Innovation Curve

In 1962, social scientist Everett M. Rogers developed a way to describe how new ideas, behaviors, or technologies gain momentum and disperse through a population.[41] Many of the innovators, developers, and marketers that followed have used his Diffusion of Innovation (DOI) curve when launching new programs and products. Rogers's innovation curve is also a useful framework for understanding how a brand-new health profession, the physician assistant, moved from idea to reality in record time. Though we weren't aware of Rogers's work at the time, it is a useful methodology to describe, in retrospect and in sociological terms, the birth of a brand-new healthcare profession.

Rogers divided his innovation curve into five phases to

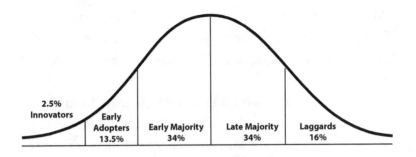

describe the different people who adopt a new idea: *innovators, early adopters, early majority, late majority*, and *laggards*.

Innovators are the pioneers, visionaries, risk-takers, and inventors who build something where nothing existed. Early adopters see a good idea taking shape and jump in, building a foundation for a wider launch. The early majority adopt a new idea once the foundation is laid. The late majority wait for a history of success before they invest. Laggards are the last to get on board.

Stead, Silver, and Smith were the innovators of the PA concept, and their pilot programs were funded by private foundations. The signs of the transition into the early adopters phase became apparent when federal health agencies began providing support and legal mavens began looking for ways to license the profession. Beginning in 1969, early adopters joined in, setting the profession on high speed to majority adoption.

As early adopters, we entered the campaign to establish the physician assistant profession when it was already well imagined but not yet fully designed. To establish a thriving program at Yale, we needed to develop a solid curriculum and make sure our graduates could practice legally. Our research at the Department of Health, Education, and

Welfare gave us a running start in both these areas, but our first class was joining the program in just six months, which didn't give us a lot of time. Fortunately, we could split up our tasks.

Fred and Paul Moson, a recent PA graduate from Duke's second class, took on the bulk of the curriculum development in collaboration with many talented members of the Yale Medical School faculty. We had a clean blackboard for putting together the content and design of the curriculum. We needed to determine how deep the learning should go in each field: medicine, surgery, pediatrics, psychiatry, and obstetrics, plus anatomy, physiology, and pharmacology. How would students understand the limits of their knowledge and recognize when to ask for more guidance? We focused on the core principles in each area. The development of an entirely new curriculum was a monumental task. Throughout the first year, our small faculty team realized that we were often writing the curriculum a week ahead of the students studying it.

During this time, we were also actively engaged in spreading the word across the country about the proposed amendment to the states' medical practice acts to permit PAs to practice.

Blair recalls

We already knew the important leaders in the American Medical Association, American Hospital Association, and HEW through our work on organ transplantation. We were able to highlight the proposed amendment's benefits to physicians and hospitals and to assuage any concerns about scope of practice and liability. They could see the amendment wasn't creating a new licensure category. Instead, it would codify a physician's right to delegate tasks to healthcare personnel working under their supervision and control. Satisfied, they gave their seal of approval.

The amendment had to be adopted in each of the fifty states if PAs were to be able to practice nationwide. The AMA legal infrastructure kicked into gear, lobbying state legislators. We also connected with the Federation of State Medical Boards (FSMB). Our colleagues, Harvey Estes and Martha Ballenger, at Duke University were solidly on board.

The amendment rapidly began to pass in state legislatures across the country because it was a simple solution to an important problem, and it had been approved by all major stakeholders before it landed in the legislators' hands. Connecticut, our new home state, adopted the amendment in 1971, just after we admitted our first class of five student PAs.

Jack Cole became particularly important to the establishment of the PA program, introducing us to leaders of established departments at Yale as the directors of the new program in town. Most professors were supportive, but we encountered some opposition. Yale's nursing school dean was opposed to the PA program before it started, and the director of the Allied Health Division wanted to take it over. Again Cole was essential in providing the support we needed to proceed.

Dick Hall shows the way

On a Friday night in 1972 at Yale New Haven Hospital, Dick Hall, a member of Yale's first PA class, was doing his rotation (clerkship) with a clinical orthopedic professor when they were called to see a victim of major auto accident. This young woman was suffering from a compound fracture of her leg, was losing blood, and clearly needed surgery. The emergency room buzzed with the frenetic energy typical of a Friday night. While the ED team prepared the patient for surgery, Dick's supervising physician asked him to take a medical history and conduct a physical examination. In her foggy condition, the woman also complained about pain in her head and, as trained, Dick started his physical exam there. He pulled his gloved hand from behind her head and saw it was covered in blood. The ER staff, in its rush to address the woman's most obvious injury, the compound fracture of her leg, had overlooked a fractured skull. Dick called over the ER chief of staff. And indeed before the patient could undergo orthopedic surgery, she needed a neurosurgeon. Having a PA student available to do a thorough exam, in that bustling emergency room, led to this patient receiving the best care.

News of the PA student who helped save a life quickly spread throughout the medical school and hospital. If anyone at Yale had questioned the value of PA students, they didn't do so again, thanks to Dick Hall.

An Opportunity for Leadership

Jack Cole also helped us find opportunities to expand our impact. In early 1971 as the PA program admitted its first class, he attended a meeting in New York with representatives from five leading private foundations that played a role in supporting the pilot programs we had visited: the Carnegie Corporation, The Commonwealth Fund, the Josiah Macy Jr. Foundation, The Rockefeller Foundation, and the Association for the Aid of Crippled Children (later renamed the Foundation for Child Development).

The PA pilot programs had demonstrated significant success, and these foundations wanted to know what they could do to help these new healthcare professionals fulfill their promise of addressing the doctor shortage, especially in primary care. They requested a position paper that analyzed the crucial organizational and credentialing challenges for the new professions and recommended next steps. Cole had two people in mind.

We gladly accepted, inviting Ann Bliss, our nursing colleague, to collaborate with us. By the end of 1971, we had completed a 100-page paper describing the pilot PA programs, the concept's promise to satisfy the nation's health manpower needs, the steps necessary for the profession to succeed, potential future obstacles, organizing principles for healthcare teams, and legal and regulatory concerns. We presented our findings and recommendations at two meetings with the foundations' leaders at The Commonwealth Fund offices in Manhattan. They asked us to turn the report into a book that they would distribute to an extensive list of contacts they hoped would become advocates for this new generation of healthcare professionals.

The book, *The Physician's Assistant—Today and Tomorrow*, was published in 1972. It became a blueprint for the PA profession. The foundations sent hundreds of copies to federal and state officials, including to every person in the US Congress, governors, chairs of state health departments, deans of medical and nursing schools, and schools of public health. Copies were sent to directors of hospitals, presidents of national organizations, and leaders of private philanthropies concerned with health issues. Here was a plan, written by a physician, a lawyer, and a nurse, about a new profession, supported by leading foundations, to help alleviate the nation's primary care practitioner shortage.[42]

The foundations that had invested risk capital during the innovator phase became instrumental, during the early adopter phase, in pushing the PA profession toward majority adoption. We knew however, that to enter majority territory and to scale the PA profession nationally, we needed to establish quality controls and norms in education, training, testing, and practice. While we were building the PA program at Yale, and in collaboration with pioneers like Stead, Estes, Smith, Silver, Ford, and Ingles, we were also helping to chart the future for the PA profession nationwide.

Building the Four Pillars

All innovations start somewhere. Their origins sometimes involve a few colleagues in a garage, basement, or dorm room. Sometimes, their trajectories cause them to become global sensations, like Hewlett Packard, Apple, or Google.

Major developments in public policy, law, and medicine have their stories too. For the PA profession, the "garage" was Duke University. There, the first program adopted the name "physician's assistant." Beginning in 1968, Duke hosted an annual conference for PA pioneers to bring together leaders and scholars to discuss issues of common concern.

The PA phenomenon had completed the innovator phase and was moving into the early adopter phase. It was ready to develop the infrastructure it needed to grow to scale. In 1972, at the fourth Duke Conference on PAs, a small group of PA program leaders began preparing for majority adoption.

Fred remembers

Many conference participants had already headed home, but eight or so of us PA program directors gathered to discuss issues about curriculum, student selection, measuring competence, and related matters. Duke had stated that this was their last national conference, but the conversation among PA educators needed to continue. The PAs themselves had established an association in 1968: American Association of Physician Assistants (AAPA), later renamed American Academy of Physician Assistants. We needed something equivalent for educators. The name chosen, Association of Physician Assistant Programs (APAP), was modeled after the Association of American Medical Colleges (AAMC). I was elected president.

Creating a Unified Profession

In addition to a solid legal foundation, all healthcare professions rely on four pillars: an association for the practitioners, an association for the programs that educate the practitioners, a system of accreditation of educational programs, and a certification system that documents that the practitioners are competent healthcare professionals. By 1972, with states adopting the amendments to their medical practice acts, the legal foundation for PAs was growing. The associations for practitioners and educators, AAPA and APAP, had been established. But we had more work to do. We still needed to build the columns for program accreditation and practitioner certification. And we needed to build them quickly.[43]

The reasons for urgency, were compelling. Funding from the 1971 federal Health Manpower Act had tripled the number of PA-like training programs, and we needed to establish standards and uniformity. As word about this up-and-coming healthcare profession spread, opportunists were taking advantage of the unregulated territory, offering to "certify" PAs after a mere two months of training, or for a mere one hundred dollars. As educational leaders, we were ethically obliged to ensure that these new medical practitioners were receiving training commensurate with their responsibilities to offer the high-quality care their patients deserved.

A legal foundation alone would not enable PAs to weave seamlessly into the fabric of the American healthcare system. To help alleviate the country's health workforce problem at scale, PAs needed to be tested and certified by a recognized national organization, just as doctors and nurses were. And

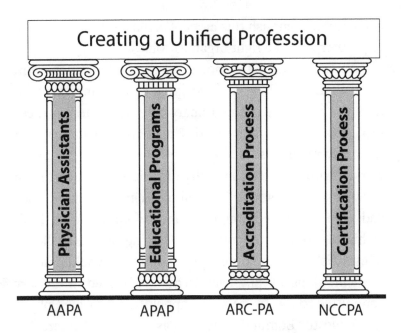

PA programs needed to be accredited by a national body, similar to medical and nursing schools. The sooner that happened, the sooner PAs could be deployed nationwide.

Finally as PA program directors, we felt responsible for fulfilling our promise to our PA students and graduates. They were the risk takers in this healthcare revolution, investing their time, energy, ingenuity, and tuition money into this profession, marching forward with the faith that a path would open ahead of them if they pressed on.

The Association of Physician Assistant Programs set ambitious goals when it hosted a first national conference for all stakeholders in the PA profession. We also wanted to establish a mechanism for accreditation of PA programs, and to devise a national test to certify PAs. APAP leadership could not accomplish this alone. Fortunately we knew how to partner with the right organizations.

We turned to the National Board of Medical Examiners (NBME) for help in developing a certifying examination for "assistants to the primary care physician," as these professionals were then called. The NBME, created in 1915 to certify medical students and medical school graduates, worked with physician specialty organizations to certify an array of specialists from internal medicine to surgery. They had never examined nonphysicians before, but their leadership realized the importance of taking on the challenge of establishing a brand-new profession that would practice medicine alongside physicians. They established an advisory committee to create the exam, appointing esteemed physician educator Edmund Pellegrino as chair and Barbara Andrew, an expert in testing from the University of Southern California, as project director. Together as members of the Advisory Committee, we created a competency-based exam, testing candidates' ability to diagnose specific conditions and perform the most important 300 tasks in primary care.

PA educators also worked with the American Medical Association to develop standards for accrediting educational programs. A Joint Review Committee on Educational Programs for the Assistant to the Primary Care Physician (JRC-PA) was established to bring together leaders from every relevant medical specialty organization to identify essential components of a rigorous, two-year, academic curriculum for PAs. Fred served as a consultant.

All of these threads braided together at the APAP's first major event in April 1973. When Dr. Charles Mullican, director of the new PA program at the Sheppard Air Force

Base, in Wichita Falls, Texas, learned we were looking for a space to hold the First Annual Conference on New Health Practitioners, he invited us to hold it there. The 252 attendees received free copies of *The Physician's Assistant—Today and Tomorrow*, provided by the five foundations. They heard updates on the medical practice act amendments process across the United States from Blair and other legal scholars. They also learned about the AMA guidelines for accreditation of PA programs.

Perhaps most profoundly, they attended a panel discussion during which NBME president Dr. John Hubbard announced that the first national certification examination would be administered in December of that year. This news received a standing ovation not only from educators who had promised their PA students an exciting—though uncertain—future, but also from PAs who had taken a leap of faith into this new career.[44]

Securing the Future of the Profession

The first annual PA conference had been a celebration, but it also caused us to realize that the APAP and AAPA needed an executive structure, an administrative staff, and a home base they could share. We needed funding to build these structures.[§] One afternoon in July 1973, Fred and Tom Piemme visited three foundations in New York, which

---

§ "Coordinating these activities was a lot of work for volunteer folks. This was before computers and fax machines. In fact, copy machines were pretty rudimentary. We were communicating through phone calls and mailing carbon copies or original documents typed on onion-skin paper. It was tough to manage an organization". In Alfred M. Sadler, Jr. and Thomas E. Piemme, "A 45-Year Partnership in Crafting a Profession and Recording its History." PA Historical Society. https://vimeo.com/198237606

pledged support of $100,000 in total. The Robert Wood Johnson Foundation provided a matching grant of $100,000.

With $200,000 (about $1.25 million in 2022 dollars), we established the first national joint office of the AAPA and APAP in Washington DC, and hired an outstanding executive director, Donald Fisher. He and this office proved vital to furthering the growth and quality of the new profession.

Also in 1974, the National Commission on Certification of Physician Assistants (NCCPA), was formed. It was made up of fourteen leading healthcare organizations plus three public members and was designed to oversee the granting of certificates to those PAs who passed the national board examination. Successful exam takers were designated "PA-C" for "physician assistant–certified." All nationally certified PAs have used this designation ever since. David Glazer, an outstanding leader from Emory University, was chosen the first Executive Director.[45]

By 1974, the future of the profession was assured. The new role of the physician assistant had already been so transformative that Fred described it as "the human equivalent of a new technology."[46] Newly accredited PA training programs were now receiving financial support from federal agencies, including HEW, Veterans Administration (as it was called then), and the armed services—a sure sign of the transition from the early adopter to early majority phase.

Two Remarkable PAs

The physician assistant profession has opened up an ever-increasing number of meaningful career opportunities for people who have made extraordinary contributions to healthcare.

Kristy Thomas and Charles Bearden are perfect examples.[4748]

Kristy Thomas

Kristy Thomas, MS, PA-C, is fulfilling the vision of PA pioneers by providing primary care to patients in rural clinics in Alaska, Nevada, and New Mexico. As of 2022, she lives in Columbus, New Mexico, on an 80-acre ranch with a menagerie of dogs, cows, horses, and roosters. She calls rural health work "not glorious, but sure as heck rewarding."

"I've dealt with many frontier emergencies throughout my career," she recalls, "some of them lifesaving. But nothing quite eclipses the experience of being the only medical provider to coordinate care for a man carrying his severed arm. In that moment, I was reminded that as a rural health PA, I must be prepared to make quick, life-or-death decisions for whomever walks in the door.

"Working as a primary care PA at a remote health clinic in rural New Mexico, I see injuries that can be just as jarring as the man holding his own limb. From locals with ranching and bull-riding trauma injuries, to the elderly battling diabetes and children with infectious diseases, each patient interaction comes with unique and sometimes unexpected challenges.

"My clinic—the most remote within a network of clinics—is situated in a town of about 1,600 inhabitants, overwhelmingly Hispanic, about three miles north of the Mexican border. It is an outpatient setting that utilizes resources from hospitals to coordinate ambulance services or summon life-flight helicopters for medical emergencies. This system operates similarly to other rural clinics and hospitals, allowing remote providers to address holistic patient needs and work largely autonomously.

"Working in literally the middle of nowhere is where I've wanted to make a difference since I decided to become a PA. After I convinced Duke University to take me on for PA school, I was passionate about using my education and skills in some of the most remote towns in rural America for folks who otherwise might not have access to affordable, high-quality care. I meant it, and that is what I do every day."

Thomas readily admits that "sacrifices and risks underline rich rewards." Her patients face economic and cultural obstacles. Most of them are uninsured and live below the poverty level, and some are undocumented immigrants. "I communicate in Spanish to patients who live on the 'island' of Columbus," she says. "For them, I'm their sole option because they cannot travel south to the border or north toward the border patrol checkpoint."

Rural medicine is not for the faint of heart. "Smaller patient populations can be more demanding on the clinician due to provider shortages and the wide range of patient problems," Thomas reports. "And," she cautions, "professional isolation is a reality. My collaborating physician works 50 miles away, but is always reachable by phone, and the next nearest clinic is about 40 miles north." Living in the community she serves, she says, makes her "somewhat of a celebrity among the locals. People want me to look at their knee in the post office. I try to keep a low profile because I don't want to get trapped in the dairy aisle at Walmart."

Despite the challenges, Thomas finds great purpose and fulfillment in her work. "Every day is a test of my skills, readiness, and endurance, but I continue because I love my community and the relationships I've built with patients, who are my neighbors and friends. It is a privilege to have their trust, and it is a privilege to be here for people in this way."

Charles Bearden

One of the nation's most remarkable physician assistants is Charles Bearden, who graduated from the first PA class at Emory University in 1973 and passed the first National Board of Medical Examiners exam for PAs that same year. The next year, he was invited to serve on the NBME Committee to validate that first competency exam and became a Fellow in the AAPA. In 1975, he was in the first group of PAs to be certified in primary care by the newly formed National Commission on Certification of Physician Assistants.

After several years in primary care and in neurosurgery, Bearden found his true calling: practicing as a PA in organ donation and transplantation. He cofounded and codirected the first organ bank in Atlanta, Georgia. For 45 years, he has been involved in virtually every aspect of organ donation and transplantation and has the distinction of being the longest-practicing organ recovery/transplant coordinator in the U.S. His responsibilities have included the evaluation of donor organs for medical and surgical suitability for transplant, the ICU management and surgical recovery of donor organs, and their preservation and transportation.

Bearden's most challenging responsibility was acting as a caregiver for the families and next of kin of donors as he obtained consent for donation.

He excelled in caring for and supporting the devastated loved ones of victims of sudden, unanticipated death. He obtained consent for donation from hundreds of families and next of kin, and coordinated more than 2,500 heart, lung, liver, kidney, pancreas, and intestinal organ transplants.

In 1982, most transplant centers in North America required the donor to be in an adjacent operating room to the recipient for their first attempts at heart, lung, or heart-lung transplants. This requirement meant that brain-dead potential donors on maximum life support needed to be transported to the transplant centers where recipients lived, unless a local, suitably matched organ became available at just the time a recipient needed it, a rare occurrence. Consent from the donor's family was also required. Despite these challenges, Bearden transferred more of these donors to recipients by air than any other transplant coordinator or organ bank in the US.

In August 1982, he flew two brain-dead lung donors to Toronto, Ontario, collaborating with Joel Cooper to successfully transplant a recipient on ECMO (extracorporeal membrane oxygenation) with sequential bilateral individual lungs. In 1983, he and his team flew donors to Ontario for the first heart-lung transplant in Canada and to Pittsburgh for the first heart-lung transplants in that pioneering center.

In 1986, Bearden coordinated the historic transplant of the first female newborn heart recipient, Baby Eve, collaborating with Leonard Bailey. Baby Eve is now happily married with three children. Bearden also had the honor of assisting in liver/kidney donor recoveries with Thomas Starzl, helping to prove that multiple organ recoveries were safe and possible.

Bearden is a member of the advisory boards of Organize and of Clinical Consulting Associates and was a participant in the 2016 White House Summit on Organ Donation and Transplantation. In 2019, he was named outstanding Civilian Physician Assistant of the Year by the AAPA Veterans Caucus "for his concern, caring, and devotion toward patients, profession, and country."

In 2020-2022, he served on the National Academies of Science, Engineering and Medicine's Committee on a Fairer and More Equitable, Cost-Effective, and Transparent System of Donor Organ Procurement, Allocation, and Distribution, tasked with reforming and improving the country's organ donation system.

He gave the 50th Anniversary Graduation Address for the 2021 Emory PA Program and became a member of the PA National Honor Society.

Lessons from the Profession

The physician assistant profession developed at remarkable speed. Several factors provided the momentum to move it forward: the national shortage of doctors, combined with a ready supply of experienced people—like military corps-men—who were willing to risk signing on to a brand-new profession, eager to collaborate in ways that disseminated solutions nationwide.

PA innovation has reached the far end of Rogers's curve and is now an integral part of healthcare. The profession's early history has much to teach us about the elements necessary to launch a solution to a pervasive social problem, and perhaps something more important to teach us about problem-solving in general: the power of interdependence.[49]

As pioneers of this new healthcare category debated how best to integrate PAs into a healthcare team, three models emerged:

Dependence: A hierarchical model with the doctor at the top, PA in the middle, and patient at the bottom.

Independence: A horizontal model, with the doctor and PA individually and equally responsible and accountable for their own patients.

Interdependence: A circular model that put the patient at the center, surrounded by a multifunctional health team addressing the patient's care.

We supported the **interdependent** model of patient-centered care in our 1972 book, and it was generally accepted.

Eugene Schneller was one of the first sociologists to study how interdependence works in practice. He saw interdependence in community health centers, where multidisciplinary teams shared the responsibility for each patient. Under this model, the team "captain" varied depending upon the patient's needs. The captain might be a physician, or it might be a PA, a psychologist, a nurse, or a social worker. Ultimately, the interdependent team is dictated not by the degree a person holds, but by the patient's needs and the individual team members' abilities. Such teams better meet the multifaceted and changing needs of patients and their families.[50]

Stephen Covey, in his 1989 book, *The 7 Habits of Highly Successful People*, wrote that **"interdependence is a higher value than independence."**[51] If we hope to address major social problems, we need high-functioning teams of multitalented collaborators with diverse perspectives, working together to build solutions. We need mavens, connectors, and salespeople willing to check their egos, put the problem in the center, and work together interdependently toward a common goal.

The Emergence of the Physician Assistant Profession, 1966–1974

1966: Medicare and Medicaid are implemented, increasing the need nationwide for healthcare practitioners.

1965–1969: Pilot programs for new health practitioners begin at Duke University, the University of Colorado, and the University of Washington.

1967: Duke University graduates its first three PAs.

1968: American Academy of Physician's Assistants (AAPA) is founded.

1969–1970: Sadlers complete a study for HEW to identify the best licensure method for PAs, recommending a delegation amendment to the medical practice act of each state—a solution rapidly adopted across the country.

1971: The Comprehensive Health Manpower Training Act (PL92-157) authorizes funding for PA education and deployment.

1971: The AMA House of Delegates adopts "Essentials for an Educational Program for the Assistant to the Primary Care Physician."

1972: The Association of Physician Assistant Programs (APAP) is established.

1972: Yale University Press publishes *The Physician's Assistant—Today and Tomorrow.*

1972: The AMA forms a Joint Review Committee on Educational Programs for the Assistant to the Primary Care Physician (JRC-PA) to begin accrediting PA programs.

1973: The National Board of Medical Examiners administers the first national certifying examination for assistants to the primary care physician, to 880 candidates.

1974: AAPA and APAP open a national joint office in Washington, DC, to serve as a central clearinghouse for information on the PA profession.

1974: The National Commission on Certification of Physician Assistants (NCCPA) is established by fourteen national health organizations to oversee the national exam and assure competency of PAs.

CHAPTER 7

Emergency Medical Care: The Neglected Public Service

Teamwork . . . is the fuel that allows common people to attain uncommon results.

—Andrew Carnegie

f you were on a basketball court in 1970, in the middle of a pickup game, and a teammate collapsed without warning, what could you have done? Hardly anyone was trained in cardiopulmonary resuscitation (CPR) in those days, so even if you knew how to check for vital signs, it is unlikely you or anyone else would have attempted chest compressions or rescue breathing. The automated external defibrillators (AEDs), now commonly seen in gyms, malls, airports, and other public spaces, did not exist.

You might have tried to call an ambulance; but without cellphones, you would have had to leave the court to find a landline, and perhaps some coins to operate it. Hopefully there would have been a phone book so you could look up "ambulance service." If you dialed that number, you would have hoped someone would answer.

Unlike the high-tech mobile medical units that 911 dispatches in 2022, a 1970 ambulance was either a station wagon with a fancy paint job, or sometimes even a hearse on loan from the local mortuary. Neither was a lifesaving medical vehicle. And the driver, who was often working alone, rarely had any medical training beyond basic first aid.

Once a patient was loaded into the back of the 1970 ambulance, there was no room for an emergency medical technician (EMT) or paramedic to administer care en route. In fact, there were no EMTs then—nor could an ambulance driver radio a dispatcher to see which medical center could best meet a patient's needs. Instead, the driver went to the nearest hospital, where the staff had no advance notice, creating yet another delay in the medical response and dramatically decreasing the patient's chances of survival.

Thousands of people lost their lives, and thousands more suffered permanent disabilities because of a lack of medical care at the scene of an emergency or on the way to a hospital. Guidelines and regulations for emergency care were in place through organizations like the American College of Surgeons, the National Academy of Sciences (NAS), the American Red Cross, and the US Department of Transportation, but few were followed. Medical schools were not yet teaching emergency medicine as a formal discipline, nor were ambulance staff or first responders part of the healthcare system. The challenge of addressing "accidental injury and death" was considered a traffic safety problem at the federal level and belonged to the Department of Transportation, not the Department of Health, Education, and Welfare. No wonder a 1966 study from the NAS called accidents "the neglected disease of modern society."[52]

During the Korean and Vietnam wars, soldiers who suffered life-threatening injuries on a battlefield were aided on the spot by skilled medical corpsmen, who used radio communication and appropriate ground and air transport to get the injured to a medical hospital prepared to receive them. This, along with other catalyzing forces, led to significant changes to emergency medical services in the United States.

The Neglected Disease

In 1966, the aforementioned landmark report *Accidental Death and Disability: The Neglected Disease of Society* was published. It reported that, in the United States, accidents were the leading cause of death for people from age one to thirty-seven, and the fourth leading cause of death for all ages. Jack Cole's focus on emergency medical services was spurred by this reality. He was also impressed by a 1969 study that estimated that mortality from US vehicular accidents alone could be reduced by 15 to 20 percent, with some 11,000 lives saved each year, with proper medical care at the accident scene or on the way to an emergency room.[53]

Cole's goal for the Yale Trauma Program was to build model systems for the care of trauma victims, calling upon the cooperation of responsible groups in government, industry, and the lay community. We set out to achieve this goal in close collaboration with Samuel B. Webb, a professor of public health and the associate director of the Yale graduate program in hospital administration.

Understanding the Problem

We began our comprehensive study of emergency medical services in Connecticut by learning everything we could about EMS in the state. We discovered that no system existed.

Connecticut had thirty-five hospitals and 179 ambulance companies, with no coordination between them at the state, regional, or community levels. Worse, no records had been kept of attempts at emergency response. That meant we knew little about the situations that responders faced, the actions they took, or their outcomes. The state's emergency response providers did not have a communication system. Its ambulance personnel were not trained in emergency medical care. Only a few ambulances met federal Department of Transportation standards. To be truly effective, emergency responders had to be equipped to deal with accidents and trauma, and with acute medical, pediatric, and psychiatric emergencies, as well as a range of non-life-threatening injuries and medical conditions.

Connecticut was an ideal place to study EMS needs and to recommend and implement solutions, because it was small enough for us to reach any location within ninety minutes, and it was a microcosm of the nationwide EMS problem. Along with Prof. Webb, we scheduled interviews with key leaders in police and fire departments, ambulance associations, hospital emergency departments, and local governments. We needed to find out what they thought was required to develop a functioning EMS system. They agreed that they would find value in regular meetings of EMS leaders, where they could communicate and collaborate in person. We formed and cochaired the first statewide EMS Advisory Committee in 1971.

We benefited substantially from visiting with physician pioneers in trauma and emergency care around the country. These included Eugene Nagel in Miami, Florida; R. Adams Cowley in Baltimore, Maryland; David Boyd in Chicago, Illinois; and Richard Crampton in Charlottesville, Virginia. Lawrence Rose, who directed the EMS research grants program in the federal Health Services and Resources Administration, provided a great overview of the beginning work in the field.

Peter Safar is widely regarded as a pioneer of emergency medicine. As an anesthesiologist at the University of Pittsburgh Medical Center, and earlier in Baltimore, he and his colleagues had developed the hospital intensive care unit, the mobile intensive care unit, and the technique of CPR, which included chest compressions and mouth-to-mouth breathing. In 1966, he was instrumental in supporting Freedom House Ambulance Services, the first Black ambulance service in Pittsburgh and the first EMS service in the country to be staffed by paramedics who had medical training beyond basic first aid. His experiences and knowledge provided invaluable background, and our visit to Pittsburgh to interview him provided inspiration for our EMS work in Connecticut.[54]

Collaborating with our colleagues allowed us to identify strengths and deficiencies in emergency care, recommend remedies for the deficiencies, set priorities, identify responsible agencies, and establish a schedule for implementing recommendations.

Between July and October 1971, we supervised and deployed nine of Webb's public-health graduate students to gather data about EMS in Connecticut through interviews, questionnaires, and surveys. They found that only 22 percent of Connecticut's ambulance services required their driver-attendant to have a Red Cross Advanced First Aid certificate. Only three ambulance services carried the essential rescue items recommended by the American College of Surgeons for emergency vehicles, and none carried the requisite first-aid supplies or medical equipment, such as oxygen, splints, medicine, or bandages. None had the basic communications capability required by the time-sensitive nature of emergency care, when the difference between life and death was often marked by minutes or even seconds.

We learned that such inefficiencies in communication also slowed the delivery of care nationwide. In 1968, a presidential commission had recommended a single emergency telephone number: 911, which AT&T declared was available, yet only a few such 911 systems had been established in Connecticut, serving only 14 percent of the population. In many parts of the state, a police officer or fire rescue team had to travel to the scene to verify that an ambulance was needed before one could be called.

Like most states, Connecticut did not have an agency responsible for planning, evaluating, and regulating the state's emergency medical services. Some minimum state standards applied to commercial ambulance services, but even these were rarely enforced. Municipal and volunteer services were completely unregulated.

The Connecticut Medical Practice Act, the same act we had used to pave the way for physician assistants to practice, provided flexibility for new types of EMS health personnel to perform certain procedures while acting under a physician's supervision and responsibility. The state's Good Samaritan legislation provided considerable protection from liability in emergency settings.

Our study was completed in 1972 through the combined efforts of the EMS Advisory Committee and our Yale Trauma Program team. We compiled our findings and recommendations into a 700-page report on building a system to deliver emergency care to all of Connecticut's citizens.

Watching for Opportunity

Most ambulance drivers were desperate for further training. How many times had they taken an injured person to the hospital, wishing they could do something more to help? Medical training had to be a part of the EMS plan for Connecticut, but we were not yet sure what the training should include.

Fortunately, just when we needed it, an orange, softcover book showed up in our office. *Emergency Care and Transportation for the Sick and Injured* was a training manual for a new category of medical professionals: emergency medical technicians (EMTs). The book was produced in 1971 by the American Academy of Orthopedic Surgeons' Committee on Injuries, and it detailed what an EMT should be able to do in an emergency situation, including how to resuscitate, respond to cardiac arrest, set a splint, stop bleeding, and address a possible head injury, in addition to other common, less-serious problems.

We designed a course based on the book, and we taught the first class of twenty ambulance personnel with the help of experts, such as an orthopedic surgeon to teach splinting and a cardiologist to teach CPR. Word about the program spread quickly. Between 1971 and 1976, nearly 6,000 ambulance personnel completed the eighty-one-hour EMT training course in Connecticut. The orange book is now in its eleventh edition, and still serves as a foundation for EMT training across the country.[55]

Sharing Results

We knew hardly anyone would benefit from our study results if that meant reading our 700-page report ; we needed a more reader-friendly version. We vetted our proposals with stakeholders, including the Medical Society, the Hospital Association, the Comprehensive Planning Directors, the Volunteer Ambulance Association, the Fire Chiefs Association, the Nurses' Association, and the Regional Medical Programs.

With their input, in late 1972, we put the finishing touches on the fifty-two-page *Emergency Medical Services in Connecticut: A Blueprint for Change.* We chose a bright-red cover to make it stand out on the desks of elected officials and community leaders, just as the orange EMT training manual had stood out on ours.

As we were completing our work on EMS in Connecticut, our next professional opportunity appeared by surprise one day in a newspaper article.

Fred remembers

On a Sunday morning in May 1972, I read The New York Times headline, "Suddenly Wealthy Johnson Foundation Maps Plans."[56] The article said the

Robert Wood Johnson Foundation, a small family foundation, had received $1 billion in Johnson & Johnson stock in the will of the late Robert Wood Johnson. It would be dedicating itself to advancing healthcare in the United States, beginning with investments of fifty-million dollars in 1972. Overnight, the RWJF had become the country's second wealthiest foundation, behind the Ford Foundation.

David Rogers, the dean of the Johns Hopkins University medical school and an outspoken advocate for advancing public health initiatives, was the RWJF's first president. Gustav Lienhard, former chairman of the executive committee at the Johnson & Johnson Company, was chairman of the board. "We don't want to just support the status quo," Rogers said in the article. "We don't want to just help people who are doing papers on another way to take out your gall bladder, and we don't want to just replace federal dollars. We could spend every dime in certain ways and not make much difference."

Rogers also said that the RWJF would emphasize decreasing health costs, enhancing physician training and that of other "health professionals, improve consumer access to healthcare, improve hospital efficiency, and the process of setting public policy on health," while looking for opportunities to "enhance preventive medicine, give physicians and other health personnel a fuller appreciation of behavioral science and managerial skills and increase the training of members of minority groups in medicine and related professions."

I handed the newspaper to Blair. "Maybe we should look into this," I said.

We were not thinking of leaving Yale. Our third class of students was enrolled in the PA program, and the EMS *Blueprint for Change* for Connecticut was just being completed. The Trauma program was succeeding in its stated goals, and The Commonwealth Fund was pleased with our progress. But we had never set out to follow a linear career path, and our strategy of following opportunity had so far led us to good results. We decided to find out more about this new foundation.

Our previous experience had taught us something about philanthropic organizations. We knew that working with foundations could be just as intellectually stimulating and rewarding as working at the National Institutes of Health or Yale University. We also knew that each foundation had a unique focus and funding strategy. How would the Robert Wood Johnson Foundation operate?

David Rogers had already recruited two of our close foundation colleagues to help start the RWJF. Margaret Mahoney, from the Carnegie Corporation, had supported our work in developing the physician assistant profession. Terrance Keenan from The Commonwealth Fund had managed the Yale Trauma Program grant and supported PA development as well. We reached out to them, and they were happy to answer our questions. They encouraged us to connect with Rogers, who was delivering a talk at Yale the very next month.

We knew of Rogers's work at Johns Hopkins, which had expanded healthcare beyond the university hospital into inner-city Baltimore and the new city of Columbia, Maryland. The Yale Trauma Program was in many ways a prototype of what Rogers advocated. We felt confident we would have plenty to discuss with him when we met after his presentation at Yale. He was dynamic, visionary, down-to-earth, and dedicated to the advancement of healthcare, just as *The New York Times* had depicted him. Soon after that meeting, we were headed to Princeton for discussions with him and other senior officers at the RWJF. At the end of that day, Rogers said, "I want you to join my team as senior officers. Can you start tomorrow?"

We had some soul-searching to do. Was this the right time and opportunity to make another big leap? It was an exciting chance to be part of the beginning of the country's biggest healthcare-focused foundation, and we could continue our medical-legal collaboration while following our passion for expanding health services in the United States. We already had trusted relationships at the foundation with Margaret Mahoney and Terrence Keenan, two people we respected deeply. In addition, David Rogers was a passionate advocate, an inclusive leader, and potentially, a supportive mentor.

On the other hand, we still felt a strong commitment and bond to the Yale PA and Trauma programs, and to the goal of building a strong EMS infrastructure for Connecticut. As we considered taking positions at the foundation, we knew we could do so only with the understanding that we could not begin until we had completed our commitment to the Trauma program.

Telling Jack Cole that we were leaving was one of the hardest things we had ever done. There were tears all around.

True to his character, he warmly encouraged us to follow this new opportunity. He understood the foundation's importance to the advancement of healthcare. We assured him we would do everything in our power to create a smooth transition.

Over the next few months, we attracted two excellent medical directors who were already at Yale: Martin Robson to lead the Trauma program and Robert Levine for the PA program. The core team of the Trauma program, including Sam Webb, remained. Ann Bliss and Paul Moson continued with the PA program, ensuring its growth and evolution. Our first class of five PAs graduated in early 1973, with the commencement speech delivered by Eugene Stead. The structure was in place for Connecticut to implement the emergency medical services plan, building a comprehensive system throughout the state.

Implementing the Plan

Connecticut's EMS system came together with a remarkable speed and magnitude. The state legislature passed Emergency Medical Services Acts in 1974 and 1975. By 1976, all of the priorities included in the *Blueprint for Change* had been addressed. An EMS Council was convened, advised by the state Department of Health. In addition to the training of 6,000 EMTs between 1971 and 1976, 155 EMT instructors were also trained, and courses were developed for EMT dispatchers.

Communications improved as well, with the establishment of eleven new EMS regions, each offering a well-publicized, central phone number to call during emergencies. By

1976, 99 percent of the state's ambulances met the professionally designated standards for supplies and equipment, up from zero percent when the Yale Trauma Program team had studied them in 1971–1972. Courses were established for emergency department physicians and nurses, most of whom had no specialized training in emergency care.

The Connecticut plan for transforming emergency medical services was just the beginning. There was still much more to do. In 1977, we published *Emergency Medical Care: The Neglected Public Service* with Sam Webb.[57] The book provided the details of this transformation and plans for the future. It was dedicated to our mentor, Jack Cole.

Donald Goldman: A life saved by a modern emergency medical system

Almost every day at 5:30 a.m., Donald Goldman, a physician in Monterey, California, could be found on the elliptical machine at his favorite gym. That's where he was in 2013, in the middle of his workout routine when, without warning, he collapsed to the floor. Fortunately, the person working out next to him happened to be an ICU nurse. She checked his pulse and didn't find one. She shouted, "Call 911!" and began CPR, while someone else grabbed the automated external defibrillator the gym had on hand. While medical assistance sped toward the scene, the nurse shocked Goldman's heart twice.

Within five minutes, the emergency medical

---

team arrived, in a large, fully equipped ambulance. They took over Goldman's care, intubating him, administering oxygen, and injecting cardiac medications, then placing him in the back of the ambulance. On the way to the hospital, one EMT notified the local emergency room of his arrival, while another tended to his care—he had to be defibrillated several more times en route.

When the ambulance pulled up to the hospital, the medical staff was ready for his arrival. They quickly determined that he had blocked coronary arteries, but that his body could not yet tolerate a surgical procedure. They admitted him to the ICU, where he remained intubated, in an induced coma, while his body was cooled to 92 degrees Fahrenheit for four days, after which he awoke safely, ready for a quadruple bypass operation. Nine years later, in 2022 at age sixty-nine, Goldman, fully recovered, is still living an active life, walking 8 to 10 miles a day.

You might be struck by Goldman's incredible luck to have an ICU nurse nearby when he collapsed. He had the luck of timing as well: his medical emergency occurred in 2013. Had he suffered his heart attack in 1970, he most certainly would have died at the gym.[58]

Emergency Medical Services in Connecticut, 1966–1977

1966: *Accidental Death and Disability: The Neglected Disease of Modern Society,* by the National Academy of Sciences, National Research Council, is published.

1966: Highway Safety Act (PL 89-564) enacted.

1969: Jack Cole establishes the Yale Trauma Program to study and improve emergency medical systems.

1970: Alfred and Blair Sadler are hired to codirect the Yale Trauma Program.

1971: The Connecticut Advisory Committee on EMS is created, incorporating essential stakeholders to develop recommendations.

1971: The Yale Trauma Program study of EMS in Connecticut launches.

1971: The American Academy of Orthopedic Surgeons publishes *Emergency Care and Transportation of the Sick and Injured,* a textbook to train EMTs in an 81-hour course.

1971: The Yale Trauma Program begins training EMTs, with 6,000 trained by 1976.

1972: The Yale Trauma Program study of Connecticut EMS sends to the Governor a comprehensive report that includes recommended changes to communications, ambulances, and training for emergency service providers.

1974: *Emergency Medical Services in Connecticut: A Blueprint for Change* is produced by the Yale Trauma Program and circulated widely in the state.

1974: The Connecticut Emergency Medical Services Act of 1974 establishes eleven EMS regions in the state and consolidates the recommendations of the Yale Trauma Program study.

1975: The Connecticut Emergency Medical Services Act of 1975 further consolidates and expands the statewide EMS program.

1977: Sadler, Sadler, and Webb publish *Emergency Medical Care: The Neglected Public Service*, describing the Connecticut experience and reviewing emerging national programs and priorities.

CHAPTER 8

EMS Goes National: The Robert Wood Johnson Foundation

The Foundation played a critical role in seizing an opportunity, providing a spark, and helping to shape the changes that produced today's emergency medical system.

—Digby Diehl, "A Look Back: The Emergency Medical Services Program"

Even before we joined the Robert Wood Johnson Foundation full time, David Rogers urged us to participate in conversations about the foundation's direction.

Blair recalls

Rogers was anxious for us to get started at RWJ, but we needed to fulfill our commitments at Yale. Fred remained with the Trauma and PA programs, and I began taking the train to Princeton, where I stayed a few days a week. During a meeting with senior staff, including David Rogers, Margaret Mahoney, and Robert Blendon (a talented health policy analyst from Johns Hopkins and HEW). We began discussing how to improve access to healthcare. I had a "lightbulb" moment. Communication was a principal feature of our plan for EMS in Connecticut. Setting up a central phone number for the public to easily access emergency care was key to effective communication.

"We've been working on an idea for the past three years that might be a good place to start," I said. I emphasized that the Connecticut plan offered a dramatic improvement in access to frontline care. "We are developing a single, seven-digit phone number in each region that will be highly publicized and published in every phone book," I explained, adding that a new 911 emergency number was being tested in several regions in the state and country and could be available for widespread use in the next few years. "Of course," I added, "the people who receive those calls need to be trained in how to handle medical emergencies. And all ambulances need radios that can connect them directly with hospital emergency rooms, so they can receive guidance from physicians there, before moving their patients."

I described the excellent training manual we were using from the American College of Orthopedic Surgeons. "All frontline ambulance drivers need to be trained as EMTs," I said. To use Malcolm Gladwell's terms, I had become the salesman for a breakthrough idea that Fred and I, along with many colleagues, had already tested in Connecticut.[*]

The practical nature of our proposals caught the attention of the RWJ leaders. It was exciting to see that the plans we were executing in Connecticut might spread across the country. The foundation next wanted to consult with leaders in EMS. Rogers asked me to assemble a group of experts for a brainstorming meeting in Princeton.

A pivotal meeting

On a warm spring day, the foundation hosted a small group of EMS pioneers, including David Boyd, who had spearheaded the effort to create trauma centers in Illinois; Eugene Nagel, who had proposed that Miami-Dade fire officials use radio voice telemetry to link a mobile intensive-care vehicle to hospital-based medical command and control; George Roderick, a communications expert from Washington, DC, who was up to date on the evolution of the new 911 number; and Jim Page, who coordinated countywide EMS efforts in Los Angeles and consulted for the television show *Emergency!* That hugely popular series portrayed paramedics as the everyday heroes they were and shifted how the American public perceived emergency medical services personnel.

---

[*] Other factors contributing to the urgency to develop an EMS system included a 1972 National Academy of Sciences study that described the federal government's failures to enforce regulations or to advance the EMS system. Representatives of leading healthcare organizations also lobbied for change. In 1973, Congress passed the EMS Systems Act, providing funding for regional EMS systems and authorizing research in emergency response techniques, devices, and methods of delivery.

Blair recalls

Early that morning, Robert Blendon and I asked this group what they would do if we had fifteen-million dollars to spend on improving emergency medical care. Within an hour, the blackboard was filled with ideas: extended training for emergency room personnel, better equipment in emergency vehicles, comprehensive training for ambulance attendants, public education initiatives to teach first aid and CPR, develop a system of designated hospital trauma centers, and improve communication systems.

When we asked them to prioritize just one idea, a vigorous debate ensued. Finally, they decided that we should prioritize improved citizen access to EMS through radio communications, facilitated by agency coordination and training.

Over the coming weeks, Blendon and I designed a detailed grant program that included all components necessary to the recipients' success. We presented the program to the foundation board, which approved it unanimously. We outsourced the program's ongoing management to the National Academy of Sciences. In April 1973, the program was formally announced by David Rogers and Philip Handler, the president of the NAS. I was appointed by Dave Rogers to run it.

Lambertville, New Jersey

Between 1963 and 1976, whenever residents of Lambertville, New Jersey, needed help in a medical emergency, for example, a heart attack, accident, or poisoning; they called 397-3131. The phone rang in Norman Scheetz's dining room. If he was at home, he answered, determined the nature of the emergency, pressed a button setting off two sirens strategically located in Lambertville, and put in a radio call to the homes of on-duty volunteers of the local rescue squad.

If Norman was away, his wife Eleanor answered the phone. Sometimes the task fell to one of their children. Scheetz didn't have more than six straight hours of sleep in all those thirteen years.

Neighboring communities used other means to summon emergency aid: in some, commercial answering services took the calls, while in others a single number rang on extension telephones in the homes of rescue squad volunteers. Upward of sixty-one emergency phone numbers appeared in the region's phone directory.

A Tale of Two Kansas Cities

In the early 1970s, the Kansas City metropolitan region had forty-five different ambulance companies. Citizens facing an emergency had to figure out which phone number to call. Travelers needing help along Highway 35 might call number after number, only to be told, "Well, if you're north of the viaduct, you're mine; but if you're south of it, you need to call someone else."

A New Approach to Emergency Care

We hoped the RWJ's emergency medical services program could solve problems like this across the country. RWJ modified typical foundation practices in several ways. When we announced the program, we told applicants exactly what they needed to do to get the money. For EMS systems to work properly, they must include collaboration, coordination, and communication, and we built those requirements into the grant requirements. According to Blendon, "We let people know they could get money if they formed a coalition."

Applicants had to demonstrate how they planned to adopt new communications technology (in 1973, this meant radios), upgrade ambulance attendants' skills, train dispatchers in basic emergency medicine, and create interagency collaboration. Recipients had to show that, within a year of funding, they planned to establish citizen access to EMS, establish a single agency in charge of EMS dispatch and communications, and open access to radio control services and phone lines. They also had to train dispatch and ambulance personnel, expand the capacity for emergency services, and work toward making the program self-sufficient in two years. RWJ was the first organization to propose a nationwide definition of a comprehensive EMS system, one based in part on the Yale Trauma Program's study in Connecticut.

The foundation also targeted direct service providers—police and fire departments, hospitals, and health departments—that were potentially spearheading EMS projects in their regions. Our goal was to bring together regional organizations to improve patient access to emergency care. We awarded grants to agencies from diverse regions with the hope of catalyzing change nationwide.

Unlike many other foundations, RWJ did not select the grant recipients alone, but instead partnered with outside organizations. For the EMS project, we contracted with the NAS to screen applicants, monitor the approved projects, and evaluate the program's impact. We received a total of 251 applications, with interest from virtually every state. Following site visits and a thorough review of the proposals by the NAS and our EMS advisory committee of fifteen national leaders, we selected forty-four applicants to receive a total of fifteen-million dollars. In the end, grants of $300,000 to $400,000 (equivalent to roughly two-million dollars in 2022) were distributed to regions in thirty-two states and Puerto Rico. The selections were announced on May 24, 1974.

The winners included the Mid-America Regional Council, based in Kansas City, Missouri; Hunterdon County in New Jersey; and the City of New Haven, Connecticut, coordinator of a collaborative partnership that included Yale New Haven Hospital and the Hospital of Saint Raphael. The good work Jack Cole had envisioned with the Yale Trauma Program continued in New Haven, and far beyond, in the form of RWJ's first national demonstration project, establishing regional emergency medical communications systems across the United States. Blair personally participated in more than thirty site visits during the four years, from areas as diverse as Indian reservations to large cities and counties, to remote rural areas.

Measuring Impact: Immediate and Lasting

The EMS Advisory Committee, NAS, and RWJ staff managed the grant program, made site visits, reviewed progress, made hardware recommendations, sponsored workshops, provided low-cost technical assistance, and offered guidance for dealing with the Federal Communications Commission. We hosted highly interactive annual meetings where grant recipients could collaborate; sharing dilemmas and problems, best practices, and solutions, and where regional leaders became the new faculty; and teaching each other what they had learned in their regions. All these activities accelerated to the speed of adoption.

By May 1975, Kansas City had one emergency number to call a central dispatch center, where operators dispatched ambulances for all organizations in Missouri and Kansas. In the first year, the time from an initial phone call to a vehicle arriving on the scene dropped by 50 percent. In addition, all ambulances were now equipped with radios connecting them with all hospitals, the dispatch center, and each other.

By 1976, Norman Scheetz and his family were no longer answering emergency calls in their dining room. Instead, Scheetz worked in a new communications center perched on a hill overlooking the county seat, shadowed by a 200-foot transmission tower. He was the region's chief dispatcher. He and his team used a sophisticated electronic system to receive calls through a single 911 number. They could dispatch ambulances from any of sixteen companies in the region, all of which maintained radio communication with the region's hospital emergency centers.[59]

David Boyd, who would later direct the federal government's EMS program, said:

The RWJ program demonstrated the concept of a regionalized, systematic approach. Now everyone understands that to create a proper system, you must have all the elements: access, central dispatch, communications, hospitals, doctors, ambulances, central coordination, integration of multiple components. Those dollars had enormous impact out there.[60]

Over the following five years, the foundation's program leveraged many millions of federal dollars to help build regional EMS across the country. At an invitational White House summit on emergency medical care, Boyd invited national leaders to review the field and to brief President Gerald Ford. During that discussion, Blair described the RWJ program and commended the government for working collaboratively with the foundation. "This is a great example of the kinds of public-private partnerships that I intend to support in my administration," President Ford replied.

When the RWJ's three-year grant program ended, 91 percent of grantees had radios in half their ambulances, and 75 percent had radios in all ambulances. The radios acted as an incentive for ambulance services to coordinate with a central dispatcher and each other: to get a radio, you had to integrate it into the larger regional system.

The program also increased the number of emergency medical personnel and upgraded their skills. In 1973, the forty-four grant regions employed 6,000 emergency medical technicians and only 240 paramedics (individuals with advanced training beyond the EMT). By 1977, nearly 26,000 EMTs served the regions, along with 3,300 paramedics—numbers that grew dramatically in subsequent years.

These numbers, however, don't accurately reflect the lasting impact of the primary requirement that grant applicants function as lead organizations capable of forming coalitions and bringing together all stakeholders. Law enforcement agencies, fire departments, civic organizations, private ambulance companies, volunteer brigades, hospitals—groups that had often worked against one another, and at best only adjacent to each other—now operated interdependently, in highly functioning systems. In reviewing the impact of the program, the NAS Advisory Committee found that the program had achieved its objectives and had a major impact on EMS development.

"Usually, we have to wait a lot longer to see ideas come to fruition," Jack Cole reflected in 1976 about the rapid adoption of regional emergency medical systems. Innovations can take years, even decades, before plans are implemented at scale.[61] Our initiative—with the Yale Trauma Program's EMS blueprint embedded into the grant requirements, the funding of multiple regional EMS projects, and a quick turnaround time for results—was built to quickly ascend the innovation curve.

Twenty-five years later, a 1999 RWJ survey revealed that forty-one of the original forty-four coalitions still served their regions.[62] We can never calculate the ripple effects those coalitions have had on their communities. How many lives were changed for the better? How many people were saved?

RWJ's commitment to regional emergency medical response systems was key to the development of EMS in America. It also demonstrated how foundations could take a model idea to national scale. Accidental injury was no longer a neglected disease, and emergency medical care was no longer a neglected public service. In evaluating the program twenty-five years later, authors James Butler and Susan Fowler concluded: "Emergency medical services are embedded securely in American communities to a degree that pioneers in the 1970s could only dream about."[63] From trained 911 dispatchers to highly skilled EMTs and paramedics, to thousands of emergency care physicians and nurses, to sophisticated ambulances that transport patients directly to trauma centers, emergency medical care is now a jewel in America's healthcare crown.

Richard Zuschlag and Acadian Ambulance Service

The history of Acadian Ambulance Service illustrates the developments of emergency ambulance services nationwide. On August 23, 1971, a headline in the *Daily Signal*, a Louisiana newspaper, announced "Police Jury Declares Ambulance Emergency." The story explained a problem common throughout Louisiana: funeral homes, which had used their hearses to provide emergency transport to hospitals, were getting out of the "ambulance" business, leaving citizens with no one to call for help in a medical emergency.

Enter twenty-three-year-old Richard Zuschlag, a Pennsylvania-born electronics expert transplanted to Cajun Country; Richard Sturlese, an accountant and occasional alligator hunter; and Roland Dugas, a hospital and community leader. Together they formed Acadian Ambulance Service, a privately owned corporation.

"We created the ambulance service because there was nothing else available," Zuschlag explains. "We decided the best way to finance it was on a subscription basis. We started in Lafayette Parish: fifteen dollars per family per year. We needed 9,000 families to get rolling. Funeral homes were going out of the ambulance business on September 1, so we set that date as a deadline." Before that deadline, Acadian ordered two ambulances, the second of which was delivered an hour before the company activated their toll-free number at their dispatch center. At midnight on September 1, 1971, Zuschlag recalls, "The two ambulances started making runs. I drove one of them."

Three years later, Acadian Ambulance Service was collaborating with the Louisiana Hospital Association, a recipient of an RWJ EMS grant, to assure that Louisiana citizens, no matter where they lived, had direct access to high-quality emergency care.

"When we began," Zuschlag recalls, "we couldn't talk to one another. All the local emergency-response agencies operated on different frequencies, and cement trucks and beer trucks had better radios than ambulances [did]. We used that seed money to begin development of one of the most sophisticated emergency communications systems in the world."[64]

By 1977, Acadian's services, integrated into a larger EMS system, reached nine parishes in the region. One hundred and twenty well-trained employees served 600,000 citizens. Acadian services have expanded to include Air Med helicopters and a national EMS training academy. The company remains fully integrated into the fabric of Louisiana's emergency response.

Their ongoing collaboration, communication, and coordination was on full display on Sunday, August 16, 1998, when a call came in about an accident on Interstate 10, in the westbound lanes of the 17-mile-long Whiskey Bay Bridge. The Acadian communications center dispatched an Air Med helicopter, a paramedic field supervisor, and two ambulances, each approaching from either end of the span. The first ambulance radioed the Louisiana State Police for permission to travel eastward against the flow of traffic in the westbound lanes. Meanwhile, approaching from behind, weaving through bottlenecked traffic, the paramedic supervisor came upon additional collisions with multiple injuries. While drivers stuck in the backup overloaded the cellphone system, rendering it useless, he accessed an emergency frequency and radioed the communications center to request more support.

Leaving his vehicle, the supervisor continued toward the original accident on foot, discovering a grisly scene: nine cars and three big rigs were tangled in a chain reaction of collisions behind a tractor trailer that had slammed into a Mercedes, both engulfed in flames. Under the thick plumes of smoke, he radioed dispatch again. What had been reported as a single accident had become a mass casualty incident.

The communications center deployed fifteen additional ground units, four helicopters, thirty-seven EMTs, the Louisiana State Police, and local firefighters. Advanced technologies enabled the helicopters to pinpoint and transmit coordinates for each of the injured along the two-and-a-half-mile-long accident scene. Acadian dispatchers used this data to provide detailed directions to reach the injured, via mobile data terminals carried in the ambulances.

"The accident was one of the worst in Louisiana history," according to Diehl. "Paramedics dealt with twenty-three separate collisions, involving ninety-six passenger vehicles and ten tractor-trailers. There were four fatalities and twenty-six people injured, seven critically. The Acadian communications center tracked patient injuries and distributed victims among eight hospitals."[65] Despite the obvious challenges of the accident location, in the middle of a one-way span on a 17-mile bridge, helicopters had airlifted all the most critical patients off the bridge within an hour of the original 911 call.

Richard Zuschlag credits the grant from RWJ for helping Acadian establish this sophisticated communications infrastructure, which would play key roles in the aftermath of Hurricane Katrina in 2005 and during the 2010 offshore oil rig disaster depicted in the film *Deepwater Horizon*.

The Broader RWJ Agenda

In 1972, Waldemar A. Nielsen published *The Big Foundations*, a criticism of big-money philanthropy. In the book, he asserted that some charitable foundations were not distributing their funds and were instead holding on to them.[66] The book stimulated a series of reforms and new regulations. This must have been on David Rogers's mind when he joined the Robert Wood Johnson Foundation, the biggest private source of development capital for healthcare improvement. Rogers made it clear right away that this foundation would operate differently.

The first of those differences was at the foundation's new digs on the Princeton University campus. RWJ had rented space in the least picturesque building on the university's property, set apart from the beautiful main campus, in a nondescript, industrial-style building that had a housed a defunct particle accelerator. "I like these rented quarters, these cinderblock walls," Rogers told *The New York Times*.[67] He further set the tone in 1972 in the RWJF's first annual report:

> It is our hope that we can be effective, wise, and compassionate in interacting with those in society seeking to better the human condition. We have an overriding belief, the conviction that human ingenuity, if given the chance, can invent practicable ways of moving toward the goals we have defined as our own—and giving that chance, in our judgment, is the appropriate and privileged role of a private philanthropic institution.[68]

RWJ's humble setting was not the most significant difference between it and other foundations. Other foundations *funded* innovations. Under Rogers' visionary direction however, RWJ *embodied* innovation in its organizational design, funding practices, and transparency. The foundation's culture was collaborative, inclusive, and nimble. Those attributes also allowed it to have a positive effect on healthcare in a short period of time. We were fortunate to be a part of it.

Inverting the Hierarchy

Typically, a foundation's elder statesmen (and they were virtually all men) held the positions of power, while young staffers did the legwork. Rogers had a different notion. He thought of RWJ as a university of ideas in healthcare, a laboratory for creating and testing solutions to real-life problems.

In those early days, we participated in formative conversations about the foundation's strategy and direction. True to his nature, Rogers wasn't telling newly minted senior officers what to do. Rather he was asking us what we thought we should do.

Our colleagues were a diverse group, many of whom were our age, with experience in the healthcare or public health arenas, and we were eager to make a difference. We invited healthcare experts to contribute to our understanding of the issues, but our actions were determined by our mission, not by old loyalties or outside influences. This was not a top-down institution.

Collaboration Was Crucial

Collaboration was baked into RWJ's plan from the beginning. Other foundations employed between 100 and 300 internal staff to manage their operations, but RWJ kept its core team small, partnering with outside agencies to manage its national grant programs. Further, RWJ planned to share its outcomes widely and transparently, publishing both its wins and its losses and offering insights about grantmaking. We didn't just do things differently; we also helped other foundations understand the anatomy of our successes and learn from our mistakes.

The Importance of Focus

At the time, big-name foundations had been under scrutiny for their spending, or holding, practices. To make sure these 501(c)(3) philanthropic organizations operated properly, foundations were required by government regulations to distribute a minimum of 4.6 percent of their assets—in RWJ's case, fifty-million dollars per year.

Some foundations went from project to project, funding those that caught their attention and met their guidelines. RWJ chose to drill down into specific problem areas (emergency medical services; the healthcare workforce shortage, particularly in primary care; physician leadership training) and from there create nationwide grant programs designed to address them.

Unless you were there, it is difficult to fully appreciate the extremely important role that Walsh McDermott played in the foundation's early years. McDermott was a traditionally trained internist turned infectious disease specialist, whose interest in public health led him to become a professor of public health at Cornell University Medical College. In 1967, he became chairman of the Board on Medicine of the NAS and was one of the founders of its successor organization, the Institute of Medicine. As an RWJ senior advisor, he became an important mentor to both of us sharing perspectives on healthcare that remain alive in our work. Perhaps our favorite McDermott-ism was his term "science-based Samaritanism," a perfect shorthand description of applying science with empathy to all care experiences ranging from an individual patient and family, to a group of patients, or to a community at large.

Fred Recalls

At the RWJF, we found ourselves again in the "catbird seat," connecting with healthcare leaders nationwide, learning from those who visited the foundation, making site visits, and collaborating with our colleagues and advisers. I helped to direct RWJ's health manpower innovations in three areas: the need for more primary training in medical schools and hospitals; the need to continue the successful Clinical Scholars program; and the continuing support of physician assistant and nurse practitioner training programs.

RWJ supported teaching-hospital residencies for general internists and general pediatricians, with a goal of producing a greater number of primary care physicians. Our consultant team and I visited committed leaders at outstanding medical centers who were eager and willing to strengthen primary care.

The RWJ's Clinical Scholars program offered two years of additional training in broader disciplines, such as public health, economics, and healthcare policy, to physicians completing their residency in a given field. This program was meant to prepare scholars to lead the charge to improve health and local and national healthcare systems. During my time at RWJ, twelve leading medical centers across the country participated in the program, which had an outside administrative base at the University of California San Francisco. Six years of working with Blair on a variety of health policy issues, had served as an on the job personal Clinical Scholars Program for me and I felt fortunate to have been the Foundation's coordinator for it.

This broader education was for physicians who wanted to improve healthcare as well as see patients, and it was completely congruent with my interests. The program continued for forty years and produced 1,300 physician leaders dedicated to transforming healthcare.[69] The RWJ program has been redesigned to include multiple healthcare professionals over a three-year period with emphasis on equity, diversity, and inclusion.

RWJ also sought to enhance physician assistant and nurse practitioner training, emphasizing collaboration or "common training" between programs. In 1974, the foundation issued a grant to Stanford University and the University of California at Davis to create a pilot program training physician assistants and nurse practitioners together. I recall visiting those schools and marveling at the quality and enthusiasm of the physician and nursing leaders at both institutions.

The foundation continued to fund the National Joint Office for the Association of Physician

Assistant Programs and the American Academy of Physician Assistants to ensure its stability and to support its central role in the new PA profession. By this time, federal grants to universities had more than tripled the number of physician assistant programs—another example of cooperating with our federal colleagues.

Robert Wood Johnson Foundation Major National Programs 1972–1976

1972: RWJ begins as a major national philanthropy with a mission to improve healthcare in America, with David Rogers as its first president.

1972: The National Academy of Sciences Committee on Emergency Medical Services concludes, "EMS is one of the weakest links in the delivery of healthcare in the nation."[70]

1972: The TV series *Emergency!* debuts, featuring LA County firefighter paramedics, increasing public awareness of emergency medical care's importance.

1973: The White House Office of Telecommunications issues a national policy statement encouraging nationwide adoption of 911 as the universal emergency call number.

1973: The Yale Trauma Program completes a comprehensive study of EMS in Connecticut, with recommendations for improvement to serve as a model for other states.

1973: Alfred and Blair Sadler join the RWJF senior team and recommend prioritizing EMS as a target for improvement.

1973: RWJ makes EMS its first national program and contracts with the NAS to help administer it; Blair Sadler is appointed to lead the program.

1973: Out of 251 applicants, the RWJ advisory committee selects EMS program grantees from forty-four regions in thirty-two states and Puerto Rico, awarding a total of fifteen-million dollars over three years to develop regional EMS systems.

1973: The Emergency Medical Services Systems Act enacted, creating a national program administered by HEW, largely based on the RWJ model.

1973–1976: RWJ provides technical assistance to forty-four grantees, who make major improvements in their regions and become new leaders in the EMS field.

1973–1976: Alfred Sadler manages the Foundation's three manpower initiatives for primary care physician training, the Clinical Scholars Program, and physician assistant-nurse practitioner innovations.

CHAPTER 9

Progress and Challenges 2022

*Our country's progress has never followed a straight line—
for every two steps forward, it often feels like we take one
step back. But I hope you'll remember that the long sweep
of America is defined by forward motion, and the course we
chart from here depends on no one person alone.*

—Adapted from President Barack Obama's Farewell speech,
January 11, 2017

Many of the healthcare solutions we helped to address five decades ago to improve organ transplantation, enhance the healthcare workforce, improve emergency medical services, and foster the growth of bioethics, remain embedded in the fabric of American healthcare well into the twenty-first century. Not surprisingly, many new challenges have emerged in these areas that need attention. Here are some selected highlights from 1967 to 2022.

Organ and Tissue Transplantation

Progress

The Uniform Anatomical Gift Act remains the nationwide legal foundation on which organ donation stands. Beyond this necessary legal framework, significant scientific and medical research have produced major improvements in tissue matching, organ preservation, surgical techniques, and immunosuppressive drugs. Notably, the anti-rejection drug, cyclosporine, was developed in 1984, followed by other methods and medications to prevent the rejection of transplanted organs. Subsequently, successful transplantations have occurred using organs from donors with the HIV or hepatitis C viruses, a development that expanded the donor pool.

For almost a decade (2010–2019), organ transplants increased every year in the United States. The lack of increase in 2019–2020 was due to the impact of the COVID-19 global pandemic. In 2020, 39,034 successful organ transplants were performed. While most transplants (87%) were from deceased donors, 5,234 kidneys came from living donors. The number of living liver donors increased to 491, due to advances in surgical techniques that have made it possible to transplant one half of the liver of a living volunteer. Despite these successes, the number of people waiting for a transplant far outpaces the supply of donors and by an increasing number each year. The United Network for Organ Sharing (UNOS) estimated that 106,734 people were waiting for donor organs (mostly kidneys) as of August 31, 2021.[71]

In general, health professionals and the public have become more comfortable with the concept of "brain death":

the moment at which a person is considered dead, even though their heart is still beating. With this evolved understanding of brain death, families of potential organ donors are able to make more informed transplantation decisions.[72] The Uniform Law Commission completed the Uniform Definition of Death Act in 1980, which was eventually adopted in virtually every state.[73] The American Academy of Neurology and the American Academy of Pediatrics established brain death guidelines for adults and children.[74][75] The Uniform Law Commission is reviewing the Uniform Definition of Death Act of 1980, and a ULC working group has been formed to revise the statute based on evolving science and ethical implications.

In 1984, Congress enacted the landmark National Organ Transplant Act (NOTA), which created a nationwide network for organ procurement and allocation. The law established the Organ Procurement and Transplantation Network (OPTN), to be operated by an independent contractor. This contract has been operated by the United Network for Organ Sharing (UNOS), which regulates all organ procurement organizations (OPOs) and certified transplant centers.[76] The existing fifty-seven OPOs are nonprofit organizations responsible for the procurement of organs for transplantation. These entities are legally charged with recovering organs from deceased donors, providing support to donor families, and professional and public education about organ donation.

While NOTA has achieved some of its goals since 1984, it has failed to make the system uniformly effective in obtaining donor organs throughout the country. A distressing fivefold variation in the performance of the country's OPOs is well documented and contributes to the widening gap between supply and demand for organs.[77] [78] [79]

Over a ten-year period, the Health Resources and Services Administration and the Institute for Healthcare Improvement collaborated on several programs that improved the effectiveness of the organ donation and transplant system, but clearly more needs to be done.[80] [81] [82] [83]

Federal efforts to reform the system made some progress in 2020 when the Department of Health and Human Services (HHS) published updated guidelines that reflect advances in transplant technology and safety, and the Centers for Medicare and Medicaid services completed policy changes aimed to increase the number of organs available for transplant. The guidelines went into effect on March 30, 2021.[84]

In October 2020, alumni of the US Digital Service published a comprehensive report, *The Costly Effects of an Outdated Organ Donation System.* According to the report, which was endorsed by six former bipartisan chief technology officers of the HHS, reforms to OPO operations, governance, and oversight could save thousands of lives and billions of dollars in taxpayer funds, along with helping to address racial disparities in our healthcare system.[85] Shortly thereafter, a House Oversight Subcommittee and the Senate Finance Committee launched an investigation into "poor performance, waste, and mismanagement in [the] organ transplant industry," devoting particular attention to the operations, finances, performance, and potential conflicts of interest of OPOs.[86] It is ongoing.

In 2021, Congress mandated a thorough review of the American transplantation system. Sponsored by the National Academy of Medicine (NAM) in conjunction with the NIH, a multidisciplinary committee held meetings and heard presentations from outside experts. Discussions focused on improving the current system and increasing accountability for all OPOs and transplant centers—with a final report completed and published in 2022. According to committee chair, Kenneth Kizer, "overall the transplant system has much work to do to improve fairness and equity in who receives an organ transplant . . . as a nation, we must do better."[87]

Challenges

The ever growing epidemic of obesity and diabetes since 1990 has led to a major increase in kidney disease and kidney failure, which in turn has increased the demand for kidney transplants. New strategies are needed to close this gap.

In 1972, Medicare was amended to cover the dialysis and kidney transplant costs of patients of any age who are suffering from end-stage renal disease. Care for patients on dialysis (the thrice-weekly therapeutic process usually required by patients awaiting kidney transplants, in addition to the costs of the transplants themselves) costs taxpayers a staggering thirty-six-billion dollars a year, or 7 percent of the nation's Medicare budget.[88] Transplants are significantly less costly than long term dialysis and provide a better quality of life for most patients.

In contrast to organ procurement, tissue procurement remains largely unregulated, resulting in serious ethical and legal issues. Tissue is often taken from deceased donors and sold to hospitals and medical organizations without the knowledge or approval of donor families. More than 1.5 million of these human tissue-related surgeries are performed in the United States each year.[89] [90] Congress has begun to address the inadequate oversight of for-profit activity by several OPOs, including the sale of human tissue inside and outside the United States.[91] As Blair stated in his testimony to the NAM review committee, if these issues are not adequately addressed, they could undermine the public's trust in our organ transplant system, which is vital to its success. He noted that a fivefold variation in performance in any other area of healthcare would not be tolerated.

David Weill, who led the lung transplant program at Stanford University for ten years said in a 2019 *Wall Street Journal* op-ed: "Nearly all transplant programs have one thing in common: Too many organs go unused, not because anything is wrong with them but because of flaws in our system."[92]

In summary, while we are saving approximately 40,000 lives a year due to the diligent work of many talented individuals and teams, about 8,000 patients die each year (twenty-two every day) while waiting for a transplant. A comprehensive, collaborative effort is needed for the transplant system to reach its full potential.

Healthcare Workforce and Access to Care
Progress

In 1969, the nation faced a serious doctor and nursing shortage that was exacerbated by several factors: the adoption of Medicare and Medicaid; too few physicians and nurses who were willing to practice in rural areas and inner cities, leading to a maldistribution of the workforce; health-care costs rising beyond the reach of the uninsured; and the underrepresentation of minorities in medical and nursing schools.

Pilot physician assistant programs were started in the late 1960s as part of the solution, and the PA profession was established in the early 1970s. PAs continue to work interdependently with physicians and as integral members of healthcare teams.

The growth of the profession has been remarkable. By January 2022, there were 284 accredited PA programs, and more than 150,000 PAs have been certified nationally.[93] [94] Numerous studies have demonstrated the quality of their work, and acceptance by patients is very high. The American PA model has been adopted in twenty other countries, with some variation, in Canada, the United Kingdom, the Netherlands, Liberia, India, Ghana, South Africa, Australia, Saudi Arabia, Germany, New Zealand, Afghanistan, Israel, Bulgaria, and Ireland.[95]

Based on criteria including job opportunities, job satisfaction, and income, in January 2021, the *US News & World Report* ranked the PA profession first across all employment categories, as well as first among jobs in healthcare. It ranked the nurse practitioner profession second among healthcare professions and third across all job categories.[96]

In recognition of the importance of team-based care, the Accreditation Council for Graduate Medical Education (ACGME) encourages residency programs for physicians to include training in teams. When physicians and others learn together, they will have a head start in practicing well together.

Challenges

The United States continues to have a health manpower shortage, even with more medical schools, increases in class sizes, and the training of hundreds of thousands of PAs and NPs to provide care. The demand for healthcare continues to increase as more people have health insurance through the Affordable Care Act. It is still difficult to attract physicians, PAs, and NPs to practice medicine in rural areas, due to the ongoing issues of underfunding and social isolation.

The percentage of minorities in the health professions remains largely unchanged since the 1960s, despite considerable funding by foundations and the federal government to help minorities advance in healthcare. For example, African Americans comprise only 3 percent of medical school students. Other ethnic minorities are underrepresented as well. The exception is the great success in enrolling women into medical schools and PA programs. Women occupy slightly more than 50 percent of medical school seats (up from less than 10 percent fifty years ago) and represent 70 percent of graduates of PA programs. Women still make up 90 percent of students in nursing and NP programs, despite attempts to attract more men into nursing.

In 1972, we recommended open dialogue between emerging and traditional healthcare professions to encourage collective problem-solving.[97] We continue to promote the fostering of **interdependence** among the professions to improve healthcare for all.

By 2021, twenty-six states had enacted laws permitting "independent practice" by nurses. It is unclear whether these laws will create a barrier to team practice.

We encourage the national organizations representing organized medicine, medical education, the PA profession, PA education, organized nursing, and nursing education to meet regularly to address areas of mutual concern such as scope of practice.

Emergency Medical Care

Progress

In 1970, with no system in place, we described emergency medical care as "the neglected public service." Fifty years later, the 911 emergency number is universally available; most telephone dispatchers are highly trained to handle medical emergencies; and, according to the US Board of Labor Statistics, more than 265,000 people are employed as EMTs and paramedics.

Ambulances have become mini hospitals on wheels, regulated by strict federal and state requirements. Medical schools and hospitals in the United States host 221 residency programs in the specialty of emergency medicine, and nearly 58,000 emergency physicians have been trained since 1972.[98] The American College of Surgeons developed rigorous guidelines for trauma centers that contributed to the designation of several Level I and Level II trauma centers, 125 of which serve pediatric patients.[99] Automated external defibrillators are easy to use and have been placed in many public places. It is estimated that they can save 1,700 lives annually.[100]

Improved health technology, like wearable devices for the elderly or disabled to call 911, can summon help faster. Other technologies, such as wristwatch-sized devices that can transmit electrocardiogram ratings, or implantable pacemakers and defibrillators, can signal the onset of a problem so others can intervene before it becomes an emergency. The building of safer cars and trucks has saved thousands of lives and prevented many more injuries. Seatbelt laws and tougher consequences for drunk driving have reduced accidental deaths on roadways.

Challenges

Many emergency care systems are understaffed and underfunded, particularly in small towns and rural areas.[101] The workforce of EMTs and paramedics remains insufficient to serve the public need. In many cases, salary levels are too low to keep them on the job for the long term, leading to high turnover rates.[102]

According to Michael Kurz, chair of the American Heart Association's Systems of Care Subcommittee: "First Aid, CPR, and AED training need to become part of a larger culture of safety within workplaces. We are certainly seeing higher public interest in this training, and our campaign calls upon decision makers in workplaces and popular public spaces such as arenas, fitness centers, hotels, and churches to place AEDs in the same locations as a fire extinguisher."[103]

Launched in 2015, "STOP THE BLEED" is a collaborative effort led by the American College of Surgeons to bring knowledge of how to control severe bleeding in an emergency, to the public. An additional scourge is the "distracted driver" who is texting on a cellphone.

The Hastings Center and Bioethics

Progress

In the five decades since its beginning, The Hastings Center has played a central role in shaping the country's thinking regarding a large range of ethical questions related to public health, healthcare, science policy, and clinical research. In the words of former NIH director Francis Collins: "Since its founding, The Hastings Center never shied away from the toughest ethical issues faced by society. Through the careful deliberations of its wise experts, The Hastings Center continues to contribute reason and reflection to our most challenging discussions."[104]

Bioethics programs have been established in virtually every medical school and at many law schools and colleges. The field of bioethics has broadened its definition to include issues of public health, environmental health, and public policy.

The Hastings Center now owns two journals. *The Hastings Center Report* is a peer-reviewed journal published six times a year, which addresses a broad range of ethical issues.[105] The Center's other journal, *Ethics & Human Research* publishes critical guidance to ensure that research is carried out with the utmost attention to ethical principles. The Center's *Bioethics Forum* blog keeps readers up to date on breaking issues.[106] In August 2021, in honor of its 50th anniversary, The Center produced a comprehensive timeline that chronicles the important progress in the bioethics field since 1946. The timeline provides a listing of public declarations on the proper treatment of human beings in research in the United States and other countries; important books and articles written on bioethics; an outline of the four presidential commissions on bioethics since 1980; and useful commentary.[107]

The Hastings Center identifies and examines ethical questions embedded in our national policy. During the COVID pandemic, it became an important source of information on how best to balance individual liberty with responsibility for the well-being of the community at large. In an age of denialism, it is vitally important to address mistrust of science.

In the early days of the COVID-19 pandemic, Hastings created an ethical framework and guidance documents which have been used by US governmental agencies, the World Health Organization, and many healthcare organizations. The Center also launched an online series of *Hastings Center Conversations*, hosted by its president, Mildred Solomon, and crafted to be useful both to bioethicists, clinicians, policymakers, patients and the public. In addition to its guidance documents, it also published a major Special Report on COVID-19, which included the perspectives of frontline health care providers navigating the earliest, tumultuous days of the pandemic.[108]

The Hastings Center continues to examine complex issues related to lifespan, health and healthcare, science and technology, and the environment.[109] [110] Fulfilling the vision of its founders, Hastings puts ethics at the center of public policy conversations and debates.

The Healthcare Landscape

As of 2022, the United States is the only developed country that does not have some form of universal healthcare. Although the Affordable Care Act extended health insurance to twenty million Americans, millions more still lack coverage. Ever rising healthcare costs too often leave the uninsured or underinsured personally bankrupted by bills from a single medical incident. The United States spends twice as much money per capita on healthcare as any other developed country, yet we rank last on many metrics used to measure healthcare outcomes.[111] [112] Studies have shown that "Medicare for All" would result in substantial savings from administrative costs.[113]

As long as doctors who become specialists and subspecialists command considerably more pay for their work, there will continue to be an inadequate number of general internists, pediatricians, and family physicians.

Most Americans agree that healthcare is a basic human right, but what does health include? Access to clean air, clean water, nourishing food, safe shelter, medical care, and opportunities to thrive are all important components of health.

Healthcare, in its broadest sense, reaches far beyond hospitals, clinics, trauma centers, and public health departments to any organization or person driven to improve the health of individuals, communities, or our planet. In this sense, a homeless shelter is a healthcare organization; the integration of mental health experts into the local police force is healthcare activism; the funding of breakfast programs for elementary school children is healthcare policy;

and a pediatrician calling public attention to an alarming increase in lead-poisoning cases in her clinic is a healthcare warrior, as was Mona Hanna-Attisha in Flint, Michigan.[114]

One does not need to direct a global organization, become the nation's top infectious disease expert, write healthcare policy, or run a national grant program to have a positive impact on the health of our communities. Even our smallest choices and actions can improve health and healthcare. A person who follows science based guidelines during a pandemic, preventing the spread of the disease, is a health advocate. A person who provides a warm meal or blanket to someone in need is a health advocate. A person who offers job training to the chronically unemployed is a health advocate. A person who teaches young children how to handle their anger and disappointment is a health advocate. A person who becomes certified in first aid, CPR, or community crisis response is a health advocate.

What if, like the original Good Samaritan, we all thought of ourselves as first responders to our collective health crisis? To which issue would you respond right now?

CHAPTER 10

Fifteen Lessons for Catalyzing Change

When you see something that is not right, you must say something. You must do something. Democracy is not a state. It is an act, and each generation must do its part to help build what we called the Beloved Community, a nation and world society at peace with itself.

—Congressman John Lewis, *The New York Times Op-Ed, July 2020*

L ewis wrote these words in the final weeks of his life. This civil rights icon, who began his social justice work beside Dr. Martin Luther King Jr., was eighty years old. Pancreatic cancer had diminished his body, but his spirit, his intensity, and his passion for equality had not dimmed. Even at the end of his life, the future of the "Beloved Community" was foremost in his mind.

President John F. Kennedy, in his final full speech, inspired our generation to ask, "How can I serve?" Lewis, in his final words, told us to ask, "How can I help?" and set as a goal to "redeem the soul of the nation."

People setting out to improve the world in the twenty-first century confront complex challenges in an era vastly different from the 1960s and 1970s. Then, it would have been hard to imagine living in a "post-truth" world of "alternative facts" and the "Big Lie." It is reasonable to ask whether the lessons we learned then and share with you here remain relevant during highly polarized and politicized times. We believe that they are, and we invite you to consider them.

1. Begin Where You Are

Some people are motivated to become involved in social action through their passion for an issue like environmental health the school-to-prison pipeline, or food scarcity.

That is what happened to Gary Cohen, a travel writer who had spent two years journeying through India. In 1984, he was shocked by the Union Carbide chemical disaster in Bhopal, India, in which a pesticide factory blew up, killing thousands of people as they slept and affecting the lives of more than 500,000 residents. Back in the United States, Cohen joined the grassroots campaign to win a National Right to Know law, which would give citizens the right to information about the toxic chemical threats in their communities. He joined an organization that also supported local environmental justice struggles against incinerators, chemical dumps, and polluting factories. When the EPA reported in 1995 that medical waste incinerators in the United States were the largest source of cancer-causing dioxin emissions and a leading source of mercury emissions, he set out to convince hospitals to address the healthcare industry's pollution, a successful campaign that has since gone global. He cofounded Health Care Without Harm, which under his leadership has grown into a leading worldwide environmental health organization addressing the climate crisis as a public health emergency.[115]

Others are drawn into social action through personal experiences. In 1955, Mamie Till-Mobley took her anguish public after her fourteen-year-old son, Emmett Till, was kidnapped, tortured, and murdered by white supremacists in Money, Mississippi. Bringing the nation's attention to her son's murder helped catalyze the civil rights movement.[116] In 1980, Candace Lightner's thirteen-year-old daughter, Cari, was killed by a drunk driver while walking to a church carnival with a friend. Candace then founded Mothers Against Drunk Driving.[117] Helen Haskell lost her fifteen-year-old son, Lewis, to a medical error. She turned her grief into founding Mothers Against Medical Error, an organization dedicated to improving healthcare safety.[118]

Some people become involved by joining an organization, such as the ACLU or Partners in Health, while others pursue employment that enables them to make a positive difference in the world. Whether you have an hour a week to volunteer, or you want to launch a new initiative in your community, or you are looking to start a career in public service, take the first step and commit to learning along the way.

2. Grow from Beginner to Expert

When you become passionate about an issue, take the time to learn what it's all about and be curious about potential solutions. The more knowledge you have, the better prepared you can be to contribute effectively to the cause you have chosen.

We agree with Malcolm Gladwell's thesis that most successful movements are propelled forward by people he calls mavens, connectors, and salespeople, and these are skills that can be learned. We can become mavens when we conduct thorough research and understand an issue from multiple perspectives. Resources abound in many communities and on the internet for people to engage in deep learning about the social challenges we face.

Connectors interact within diverse networks of change agents who share resources and help each other work toward common goals. We become connectors when we build genuine, trusting relationships with people and commit to serving the greater good.

We become salespeople when we effectively express passion and communicate clearly, bringing others along to support our causes. To become effective salespeople, we must demonstrate that we are authentic, dedicated, and eager to learn.

3. Find and Develop Your Voice

Finding and developing your voice, whether through speaking or writing, can make a profound difference. You do not need to become a world-class orator or a contender for the Nobel Prize in Literature; but being able to present your ideas, concerns, goals, and needs effectively to multiple audiences better prepares you to advocate for the causes closest to your heart. Amanda Gorman found her voice on a cold January Inauguration Day for all the world to hear and appreciate.

4. Find Partners

Important progress occurs when people and organizations combine their resources and talents to work toward a common goal.

The right partners can support each other in many ways. They may problem solve by bringing together complementary skills, unique resources, or diverse perspectives. They can educate each other by acting as listeners or offering constructive feedback. They can delegate tasks and share workloads. They can help each other adjust perspectives when the stakes are high, encourage each other, and let each other blow off steam. They can celebrate wins, big and small, and comfort each other in loss.

We can seek partnerships at work, at home, or in community organizations. We can find partners among our coworkers, families, friends, and acquaintances. The right partners make us more than the sum of our individual parts.

5. Foster Collaboration

Too often, collective efforts are derailed by ego battles, territorialism, or conflicting ideologies. How do we foster collaborations in which everyone recognizes the expertise of those in the room, listens actively to all ideas, interacts respectfully, and stays focused on solving the problem?

A highly functioning, interdependent medical team is a perfect model for collaboration. An interdependent team puts the patient in the center, and leadership is based on the patient's needs. Sometimes the patient needs a doctor, sometimes a nurse, PA, pharmacist, or social worker. All parties contribute their perspectives, and leadership and responsibilities shift with the patient's needs. A working team, in any endeavor, can do the same.

We understand that competition can sometimes be the fuel that accelerates progress and breaks barriers. The American goal to land a man on the moon and return him safely to earth was clearly stimulated by our intense competition with the Soviet Union during the Cold War. In contrast, the extraordinary public and private collaboration that produced several effective COVID-19 vaccines in record time is a monument to collaboration.

6. Lead from any Chair

A person does not need to oversee an organization, initiative, or team to have a meaningful impact. When people bring their skills, talents, and perspectives to the table, they can lead from any chair.[119] This does not mean "take over the meeting" or "prove your worth." To us, "leading from any chair" means sharing what you see, offering what you have, and having the courage to step forward, all in the interest of helping your group or organization move closer to its shared goals.

The ability to lead from any chair may depend on the culture of the organization. A rigid, hierarchical culture offers fewer opportunities for people who are not designated as formal leaders to speak up and make a difference. More open cultures make opportunities more possible. When you take ownership of your team's mission, you can drive positive change from virtually anywhere.

7. Sometimes, Persistence Is the Only Option

Shirley Chisholm, the first African American US congresswoman, said, "If they don't give you a seat at the table, bring a folding chair."[120] Progress requires persistence: knocking on doors, finding allies, asking favors, taking risks, pushing past internal and external barriers, and breaking down seemingly impossible challenges into manageable steps, then walking boldly forward, flanked by your partners.

Whether you are working to gain access to existing resources, to enter powerful institutions, to get attention and support for a community initiative, or to build a coalition of your own, it is essential to remember that purpose feeds persistence, giving us the courage, energy, and motivation to move forward against the odds, in service of a higher goal.

8. Invite all Stakeholders

If we hope to create innovative, effective solutions to complex social problems, and then gain broad support, all stakeholders should be included, and their contributions welcomed, wherever possible. Including key stakeholders was essential to the success of the Uniform Anatomical Gift Act and in the development of a statewide emergency medical plan for Connecticut.

Ideally, representatives from all communities, organizations, and agencies involved in a problem are invited to help reach solutions. In today's polarized environment, some stakeholders may not be willing to participate, but it is important to try to understand their motivations and concerns, anticipate their resistance, and address them strategically.

When you find yourself at a table of decision-makers, look around and ask, "Who is missing? Who else should we invite?"

9. Seek out Mentors

Finding a mentor starts with having the courage to ask: for guidance, for an expert opinion about an idea you have, for someone's opinion about a goal you want to reach. Look around for someone who can help—and ask.

A conversation or two can open doors to new opportunities, especially when we connect with mentors who share common interests, passions, and goals, and especially when we seek help not for personal gain but to improve the lives of people in our communities.

10. Keep Your Eyes Open: An Opportunity Will Often Appear

The world often seems filled with just-missed opportunities. Developing a natural orientation towards discovery and the pursuit of possibilities can be life changing.

When Fred and his surgical colleagues at Penn were discussing opportunities in the US Public Health Service, he learned that former Surgeon General Luther Terry had become vice president for health affairs at the University of Pennsylvania, right in our own back yard. Our visit with Terry led to us working as a medical-legal team at the NIH.

When Blair introduced himself to Chief Justice Earl Warren at the squash courts, their conversation started with an overview of the game. It soon led to our work on organ donation and then to a pair of unforgettable private luncheons with the chief justice in his Supreme Court chambers, where we discussed *Brown v. Board of Education* and his successful efforts to achieve a unanimous opinion.

When Fred visited Yale Medical School on behalf of the NIH, he called upon Jack Cole, who had become chairman of the surgery department at Yale Medical School. That led to Cole's invitation to lead the Yale Trauma Program and explore the neglected world of emergency medical services.

When we read about the creation of the Robert Wood Johnson Foundation, it opened our eyes to an opportunity in philanthropy, which enabled us to participate in a whole new world of possibilities for social change.

11. When Your Path Is Blocked, Change Course

In the early 1960s, when Eugene Stead and Thelma Ingles at Duke wanted to build on the healthcare experience of highly trained nurses to create a new civilian healthcare career, they were twice rejected by the National League for Nursing, nursing's credentialing organization. Stead subsequently chose a different path, selecting highly skilled returning military corpsmen. Along with other pioneers like Henry Silver and Richard Smith, he began to test the feasibility of creating a brand-new profession: the physician assistant.

Gary Cohen was a climate advocate who was confronted by a hostile federal government following the 2016 election. He changed course and focused on progressive state legislatures and improved healthcare systems. Since 2020, Federal support for addressing climate change has increased significantly. The overall momentum of progress continues.

12. When Solving a Complex Problem, the Simplest Solution Is Often the Best

When we were drafting the Uniform Anatomical Gift Act, numerous medical, legal, and ethical questions were raised. Whether and how to define the emerging concept of brain death was just one example. Addressing and resolving these questions individually would have taken months and might have made it impossible to secure agreement. We stayed focused on one goal: to create a simple, legally enforceable statute that allowed a person to be an organ donor and that defined the role of specific family members in granting permission to donate organs when the individual had not expressed their intention. Due to its simplicity and its grounding in core American values such as altruism, autonomy, and trust, the Act was adopted in three years, with little or no change, in all fifty states and the District of Columbia.

When Roger Egeberg, HEW secretary, first asked us to develop a solution to credentialing new health professionals such as physician assistants, we soon discovered that the traditional path of creating a new licensure category had been closed. With Harvey Estes and Martha Ballenger at Duke, we realized that a simple amendment to each state's medical practice act could provide the authority for physician assistants to treat patients. With the enthusiastic support of organized medicine and hospitals, this type of amendment was adopted by virtually every state in record time.

13. Act with Transparency and Build Trust

Trust and transparency are the bedrock of healthy relationships. Transparency means acting with honesty: being clear with people about what you do and do not know, telling the truth when you make a mistake, and seeking to repair those mistakes.

Without transparency, there can be no trust. In the same way, trust can't exist without integrity, the fulfilling of our duties, and making good on our promises. Trust also depends upon sincere efforts to understand cultural and historical barriers and working to dismantle any that exist.

14. Take the Road Less Traveled

It is easy to feel pressured into established employment tracks, steered by cultural expectations, family responsibilities, or financial necessity. If taking a traditional path limits our abilities to do the work we feel called to do, or does not lead where we want to go, we must consider a less traveled path, or one we forge on our own.

In our careers or our lives outside of work, stepping off the beaten path into unknown territory can seem risky. Yet risk can reap unseen rewards, for ourselves and for our communities. After all, if today's problems could be solved by walking the beaten path, those problems probably would have been solved a long time ago.

Donald Berwick is a clear example of someone who took a road less traveled. After completing his pediatric training in Boston and in his first job, he was struck by the systemic inefficiencies and redundancies in healthcare that made life unnecessarily difficult for patients and families, often causing errors. Realizing he needed to look outside medicine for answers, he and a group of colleagues founded the Institute for Healthcare Improvement (IHI) in 1991, with the goal of reducing avoidable errors and unnecessary harm to patients. The Institute is now the world's leading healthcare quality-improvement organization.

15. Dwell in possibility

In their remarkable book *The Art of Possibility*, Rosamund and Benjamin Zander describe how living in "possibility" can transform one's professional and personal life. This "possibility" perspective is essential to meaningful social transformation as well.

It takes effort to develop a "possibility" mindset: to wonder, brainstorm, presume abundance instead of scarcity, and to imagine barriers removed. But the effort pays off: this attitude allows us to identify targets of opportunity where significant change can take root.

There will always be barriers to social progress, but there will also be opportunities to create significant, positive change. We never know when the next catalytic event will occur, energizing large-scale program development and policy change. We do not need to wait for the right time to get started. Even in times of great contention and resistance, a belief that meaningful change is still possible lets us move forward with a focus on what we *can* get done.

Visualizing an end goal—a roof for every person, nourishing food for every child, equal access to healthcare for everyone—prompts us to look for opportunities to realize that goal. We ask what resources are available and identify our potential collaborators. We determine what action steps we can take to reach that goal. Finding the courage to ask these questions can open the doors to surprising opportunities.

Can we end world hunger, solve the climate crisis, and eliminate systemic racism? Perhaps not in our lifetimes, and certainly not by acting alone. Can we make a lasting, positive impact in a particular area of concern? Considering the multifaceted crises confronting humankind, it is clear that we must. Even in the most current challenging times, we remain confident in the possibility of positive change.

As Amanda Gorman, the poet at President Joseph Biden's 2021 inauguration, said, "There is always light, if only we are brave enough to see it, if only we are brave enough to be it."[121]

Epilogue

Exploring New Possibilities

Every day I remind myself that my inner and outer life are based on the labors of other men, living and dead, and that I must exert myself in order to give in the same measure as I have received and am still receiving.

—Albert Einstein, "The World As I See It"

We worked together as a medical-legal team between 1967 and 1976, helping to usher in several large-scale shifts in the practice and delivery of healthcare services in the United States. We are grateful for the opportunities we had, the people we met, and the places we found ourselves. After nine years working as a medical-legal team, our professional roads diverged, and we found new ways to help our communities.

Fred recalls

I was excited by the work Blair and I were doing, and I was enthralled by my assignments at the Robert Wood Johnson Foundation, but for years I had wondered when I would return to my medical training. My work for the RWJF had me touring medical centers around the country, visiting recipients of the foundation's primary care residency grants, and that experience made my question seem more insistent and immediate.

I had stepped off the clinical track at the end of my surgical internship. Watching these young interns and residents work with their patients, particularly in primary care, I was reminded of why I had been attracted to medicine in the first place. I wanted to create ongoing relationships with patients that allowed me to attend to the whole person.

During my third year at the foundation, I was accepted into the internship class in the primary care track in internal medicine at Massachusetts General Hospital and the Harvard Primary Care Program, which included like-minded interns and residents from Harvard's other teaching hospitals.

Reentering clinical studies after a nine-year break was daunting. My patient-care skills were rusty, and many new diagnoses and treatments had been developed while I was away from the bedside. I left RWJ in the spring of 1976, a few months before my internship began, to give myself the chance to study medical texts and journals and to refresh my clinical skills with the help of several young physician mentors.

This next phase of my career was different in some ways. Unlike the uncharted territory Blair and I explored together, this path was well worn. I traveled with a cadre of bright young colleagues (at age thirty-five, I was considered the old guy) and a world-class faculty. It was stimulating, exhilarating, exhausting, and at times downright frightening, but I always had a collaborative team to address the most difficult patient problems, from the clinic to the ER to the ICU.

Medical training is team-based care, learning from the people ahead of you and helping teach the cohort behind you. I will always be grateful to Alexander Leaf, chairman of the Department of Medicine, and John Stoeckle, chief of the outpatient clinics and neighborhood health centers. Martin Mihm in dermatology was particularly inspiring. Robert Lawrence and Katherine Fleischmann directed the Harvard Primary Care Program. My colleagues in training included James Richter, John Mickey, Jerome Groopman, Albert Mulley, Allan Gorroll, David Blumenthal, Mark Fishman, Martin Samuels, and Amy Pruitt, to single out a few of the outstanding group from whom I learned much.

I completed my three-year internship and residency in July 1979, and I accepted an offer from UCLA Medical School to help launch a program in geriatric medicine, as a tenured associate professor. I was fortunate to work with David Solomon, John Beck, Kenneth Shine, and Robert Brook, among other outstanding leaders.

I soon discovered that the administrative duties of running a new division consumed most of my time, leaving little for the direct patient care I sought. A colleague suggested I visit Monterey County, on the central California coast, and I fell in love instantly with its breathtaking natural beauty. Featured in John Steinbeck's novel, East of Eden, Monterey County still reflects the cultural divide the author described 100 years ago, with the mostly well-off inhabitants of the peninsula towns of Carmel, Pebble Beach, Monterey, and Pacific Grove on one side, and the mostly Hispanic agricultural workers in the communities of the Salinas Valley on the other.

For my first decade there, I was a physician in the private

practice of general internal medicine with three other internists in Monterey, working in both office and hospital care. I immediately saw a need to expand healthcare access throughout the county, and established a clinic with a PA in the nearby town of Marina, which had no primary care for its underinsured and underserved population. After directing the clinic for eight years, serving mostly as a volunteer, I turned it over to the Monterey County Health Department, which continues to manage it as of 2022.

In 1993, I took on the leadership of an urgent care and primary care center in Salinas, as a physician and medical director. Urgent care has emerged over the past four decades as a hybrid between primary care and emergency medicine. It offers a place for patients to be seen for significant illnesses and non-life-threatening injuries that need immediate attention. We were open thirteen hours a day, seven days a week, every day of the year. We supervised PA students from Stanford and NP students from San Jose State. Learning some Spanish helped me connect with patients and families during this twenty-five-year effort to help address the medical needs of this largely underserved community.

In my years in practice, I have been distressed by the ever-expanding scourge of addiction, which has grown far beyond alcohol to include various drugs (some, like opiates, prescribed, and many sold illegally), gambling, sex, pornography, and even social media. Twelve-step programs based on Alcoholics Anonymous remain essential to the solution, but additional approaches are needed (which are beyond the scope of this epilogue).[122][123][124]

Many physician, PA, and nursing colleagues are exemplars of capable and compassionate care, including Lee

Goldman, Geraldine Taplin, John Morrison, Terrance Moran, Lane Verlenden, Eric Jacobson, Roger Shiffman, Donald Goldman, Yvonne Torrez, Richard Gilliam, and Stephen Panattoni. I could mention many others. Faith Fitzgerald and George Meyer, my esteemed colleagues from the American College of Physicians, Northern California Chapter and UC Davis, served as inspirational teachers. I have lost count of the many patients I helped take care of during nearly four decades of practice, but I remember many of them who warmed my heart.

My seventeen years in Toastmasters, with a home Club of the Naval Postgraduate School in Monterey, has enriched my life in so many ways. Written communication is taught in school, but effective oral communication is not. In addition to my own benefit, I have had the pleasure of mentoring many others in the quest to find their voices.

The Breakthrough Men's Community Program, founded by renowned psychologist, Fred Jealous in Monterey in 1991, has provided deeper insights into core issues facing all men. I have found it to be a powerful program for deepening understanding of men's issues across ages and backgrounds.

The increasing administrative burdens placed on all physicians, particularly primary care physicians, have taken the joy out of medicine. In my last years of practice, the insertion of the electronic medical record slowed our work. While EMR has benefits for billing and sometimes reduces errors, it has limited the joy of taking care of patients.

By continuing to play squash and tennis, I have kept active and given myself the present of arthritic knees. I have learned to say "good shot" when what I really mean is that the ball was out of my reach.

I have remained active in supporting the PA profession, serving as president of the Physician Assistant History Society and writing articles and books on the history and evolution of the field. I enjoy teaching at other PA programs and giving inaugural and commencement addresses. Getting to know the next generation of students brings me great joy and high expectations for the success of this profession in helping to serve patients effectively.

Beginning in 2013, I helped create a new PA program at nearby California State University, Monterey Bay, which trains master-level physician assistant students in a twenty-eight-month program focused on providing health practitioners to treat underserved populations for Monterey and neighboring counties. In spite of the severe restrictions put in place by COVID, we were able to graduate our first class of twenty-nine freshly minted PAs in May 2021, each of whom passed their National PA Board Examination. More than half are working in the tri-county area. Collaboration with faculty and physicians in the community allows me to pursue the goal of "science-based Samaritanism." I look forward to celebrating the fiftieth anniversary of the Physician Assistant Education Association (PAEA) and of the Yale PA Program.

Medicine is a calling with many incarnations, and I feel fortunate to have participated in a few.

Blair recalls

I stayed at RWJ for a year after Fred left, leading the EMS program, directing the Health Policy Fellows program, and with Walsh McDermott managing the foundation's national program in regional perinatal systems. By my fourth year, the EMS program was coming to a successful conclusion, and I realized it was time for a career change.

I talked with Dave Rogers about my next move. He enjoyed acting as a sounding board, advisor, and mentor, and he enthusiastically offered to help. Soon after our conversation, he received a call from Charles Edwards, who had been the commissioner of the FDA under President Richard Nixon. Edwards was about to become president and CEO of Scripps Clinic and Research Foundation, in California, and he was searching for a vice president and director of its hospital and clinics. He wondered if Rogers had someone to recommend.

Minutes later, Rogers walked into my office with a smile. "You're going to hear from Charlie Edwards," he said. Sure enough, Edwards called. I met with him, personally and subsequently with the Scripps leadership through a series of interviews and moved to San Diego to begin my adventure in hospital leadership and management.

In 1980, after three years at Scripps, a colleague encouraged me to apply to become the new president and CEO of San Diego's Children's Hospital. The opportunity to work with children and their families was irresistible. Within a week, I had interviewed for the job, accepted the offer, and began my next journey. This one lasted twenty-six years.

My new position embodied my commitment to children's health and safer communities, an opportunity to connect with the larger San Diego community, and the chance to collaborate with colleagues, philanthropists, researchers, politicians, journalists, and social policy makers. It offered a focus on the future that I believed could offer a lifetime of career excitement and engagement, and it did.

My tenure at Children's started off with a crisis. Three babies in the neonatal intensive care unit (NICU) suddenly and inexplicably died. I immediately created a crisis management team to discover and eradicate the cause. We went public each day, sharing what we did and did not know. Ultimately, we discovered that a bacterium was transmitted through the air-handling systems in the NICU—a first in an American hospital. Children's Hospital subsequently received accolades from the media, including the Diogenes Award for clear and transparent communication, and an increase in the community's trust, based on our empathy and honesty. These qualities became hallmarks of our culture.[125]

In 1980, Children's had only 107 beds, focused on caring for the region's sickest children. I worked to form collaborative relationships with physicians and other hospitals in the region that had their own small pediatric units. By 1984, Children's was selected as the sole designated pediatric trauma center for the region by the American College of Surgeons and San Diego County. My previous experience at the Yale Trauma Program and the Robert Wood Johnson Foundation were very helpful in advocating on behalf of Children's to achieve this important designation.

In 2001, after eighteen years of negotiations and four failed attempts, Children's and the University of California San Diego signed a long-term affiliation agreement to combine pediatric programs and collaborate in teaching and research. David Bailey, the fifth dean of the UCSD medical school with whom I worked, was an instrumental visionary in making this partnership happen.

The hospital, renamed Rady Children's Hospital after a very generous gift from Ernest and Evelyn Rady in 2006, has

550 beds, is the largest pediatric hospital in California, and treats more than 90 percent of the region's children from birth to age fourteen. The core of this success was our unfailing commitment to collaboration and partnerships.

Part of our mission of improving the health and safety of San Diego's children involved routinely engaging in discussions focused on identifying and addressing issues that adversely affected children. The tragedy of child abuse was commonly discussed. In 1980, renowned pediatrician and medical director, David Chadwick, and I asked the hospital board for the financial support to launch a new center focused solely on reducing child abuse. The Chadwick Center for Children and Families has become one of the leading interdisciplinary centers in the world focused on eliminating child abuse.

In the early 1990s, Children's built a new patient care pavilion. I wanted to be sure we took into consideration the experience of patients and their families at the hospital. I was equally committed to incorporating the psychological and sociological elements known to help children and families coping with illness. We paid close attention to the latest research into how the physical environment—including arts and music programs—affected patient care. The pavilion opened in January 1993 and won numerous awards for its innovative and calming design. Expanding on this theme, Children's was the country's first pediatric hospital to build a healing garden. It now has five.

I continued to advocate for evidence-based healing design as a board member of the Center for Health Design. In collaboration with a multidisciplinary team, including leading hospital architects, we designed an imaginary hospital, called the "Fable Hospital," and published articles that rigorously analyzed the costs and benefits of evidence-based healthcare design to patients, families, and staff. Derek Parker, Len Berry, Robin Guenther, and Kirk Hamilton have been great colleagues in this work.[126] [127]

In the late 1990s, under increasing pressure from insurance carriers to prove quality of care, my colleagues and I created the nation's first Center for Quality Improvement in a children's hospital, recruiting Paul Kurten to lead it. Rady Children's was the first pediatric hospital in the nation to receive the Ernest A. Codman Award for our work in quality improvement and clinical pathways. We helped form the Child Health Accountability Initiative, now a national patient-safety initiative involving more than 100 pediatric hospitals.[128] During this time, I devoted considerable time to learning the science of quality improvement and encouraged others to do the same.[129]

We created the first Center for Healthier Communities in a children's hospital. Over the past three decades, under the able leadership of Cheri Fidler, this center developed partnerships with schools, community organizations, and San Diego County to improve the social determinants of health. As the director of the county's Department of Health and Human Services and as a pediatrician, Robert Ross was a superb partner.

As the only children's hospital located on the US-Mexico border, we had the unique opportunity and obligation to collaborate with our colleagues in Tijuana. As a presidentially appointed member of the US-Mexico Border Health Commission, I had the opportunity to become immersed in the vast need for improved care along our border with Mexico.

Throughout my tenure, I had the benefit of working with an extraordinary number of able trustees, dedicated physicians, staff, and an army of volunteers. Our core management team of Meg Norton, Roger Roux, Paul Van Dolah, David Gillig, Buzz Kaufman, Barbara Ryan, and Charles Wilson were outstanding partners. We also benefited from developing superb working relationships with federal, state, and local politicians, and I spent considerable time advocating for improved policies supporting children and youth.

I retired from Children's in 2006, but I have remained involved in improving healthcare, serving as a Senior Fellow and faculty at the Institute for Healthcare Improvement, which has been a rewarding experience. Don Berwick and Maureen Bisognano are superb, generous leaders and collaborators. It is an honor to be part of the IHI Senior Fellows and Fellows networks.

I served on The Hastings Center Board for ten years, and (after a two-year hiatus) have rejoined it. Tom Murray and Millie Solomon have been innovative leaders and the talented Hastings scholars are breaking new ground in the knowledge and awareness of ethical issues. As a board member of Health Care Without Harm, I helped design a national campaign, patterned on the IHI 100,000 Lives Campaign, enrolling more than 2,000 hospitals to develop healthier environmental practices in medical facilities.[130] Gary Cohen has developed a remarkable organization that is leading the way toward the goal of successfully connecting health and climate change.

Through teaching at the innovative UCSD Rady School of Management, extensive writing, and giving presentations internationally, I remain a passionate advocate for evidence-based architectural design, healing arts in health-care, transforming healthcare's environmental impact, and leading with transparency and empathy in times of crisis.[131] [132] The late Jim Conway, Kevin Stewart, Tom Gallagher, and Alide Chase have been superb partners in advancing the cause of leading with transparency.[133]

In 2006, I joined the newly formed board of San Diego's Access Youth Academy, a nonprofit after-school program that begins in middle school with the goal of helping underserved students become the first in their families to complete college. Access Youth Academy combines individualized academic enrichment, health and wellness training, community engagement, and leadership skills development with the sport of squash.[134]

Since 2010, I have served as chair of the board, with the goal of building a state-of-the-art education and squash facility that could serve many more youth. After more than ten years, we were able to build an exciting new facility located in a federally designated Promise Zone in southeast San Diego, which opened in July 2021. Working hand in glove with Renato Paiva, our dynamic young executive director, Access has developed partnerships with sixteen schools. Our program is now able to help significantly more children live healthier lives, benefit from college educations, and understand the importance of giving forward to one's community.

A Return to Active Collaboration

Over the past decade, we have found ways to renew our partnership. In 2012, we returned to Yale to celebrate the fortieth anniversary of the Yale PA program, and we joined the advisory board of Organize to help spur the continued growth and success of organ donation and transplantation. In 2016, we participated in a White House summit on organ transplantation and gave a presentation at the 2018 annual meeting of the Uniform Law Commission on the history of the Uniform Anatomical Gift Act, as part of a celebration of its fiftieth anniversary.[135]

We have written about the fifty-year history of the UAGA and the importance of its core principles for *The Hastings Center Report* and the *Bioethics Forum*.[136][137] We have contributed to the continuing debate over the advantages of "opting in" versus "opting out" for the *British Medical Journal*.[138] As Hastings Center Fellows, we helped celebrate the Center's fiftieth anniversary in 2019 and helped provide a history of its early days.

The partnership continues.

Endnotes

1. Brian West and Matthew Varacallo. "Good Samaritan Laws." (Treasure Island, FL: StatPearls Publishing LLC, 2019). https://www.ncbi.nlm.nih.gov/books/NBK542176/
2. History of the Surgeon General's Report on Smoking and Health, Centers for Disease Control and Prevention. (Office on Smoking and Health. Oct 19, 2021). https://www.cdc.gov/tobacco/data_statistics/sgr/history/index.htm
3. Cyril Wecht, Ethan Allen Turshen, and William R. Rule. Ed. Philip A. Faix. *The Medico-Legal Autopsy Laws of the Fifty States and the District of Columbia* (Arlington, VA: American Registry of Pathology, Armed Forces Institute of Pathology, 1966).
4. Christiaan Barnard, "Human Cardiac Transplantation: An Evaluation of the First Two Operations Performed at the Groote Schur Hospital, Cape Town," *American Journal of Cardiology* 22 (1968): 584–596.
5. Health Resources & Services Administration, "Timeline of Historical Events and Significant Milestones" (April, 2021) www.organdonor.gov/about/facts-terms/history.html
6. National Conference on Uniform State Laws, Uniform Anatomical Gift Act (1968).
7. Alfred M. Sadler, Jr. and Blair L. Sadler, "Transplantation and the Law: The Need for Organized Sensitivity" (*Georgetown Law Journal* 57, 1968): 5–54.
8. Alfred M. Sadler, Jr., Blair L. Sadler, and E. Blythe Stason, "The Uniform Anatomical Gift Act: A Model for Reform," *Journal of the American Medical Association* 206 (1968): 2501–2506.
9. Ad Hoc Committee of the Harvard Medical School to Examine the Definition of Brain Death, "A Definition of Irreversible Coma," *Journal of the American Medical Association* 205 (1968): 337–340.

10. Jesse Dukeminier and David Sanders, "Organ Transplantation: A Proposal for Routine Salvaging of Cadaver Organs," *New England Journal of Medicine* 279 (1968): 413–419.

11. Alfred M. Sadler, Jr., Blair L. Sadler, E. Blythe Stason, and Delford L. Stickel, "Transplantation—A Case for Consent," *New England Journal of Medicine* 280 (1969): 862–867.

12. The Ad Hoc Committee on Medical-Legal Problems reported to the National Academy of Sciences' National Research Council Committee on Tissue Transplantation.

13. Alfred M. Sadler, Jr., Blair L. Sadler, and George E. Schreiner, "A Uniform Card for Organ and Tissue Donation," *Modern Medicine* 37 (1969): 20–23.

14. Reg Green, "Opinion: 'The Nicholas Effect' 25 Years Later. After We Donated Our Son's Organs, Italy Was Never the Same," *Los Angeles Times* (Sept 29, 2019).

15. The Nicholas Green Foundation (2020). https://nicholasgreen.org/about

16. Kenneth Moritsugu, personal communication (2020).

17. Greg Segal, personal communication (2020).

18. Henry K. Beecher, "Ethics of Clinical Research," *New England Journal of Medicine* 274 (1966): 1354–60.

19. Jean Heller, "Syphilis Victims in the U.S. Study Went Untreated For 40 Years", *The New York Times* (July 26, 1972): 1,8.

20. Paul Ramsey, *The Patient as a Person.* (New Haven: Yale University Press, 1970).

21. Hans Jonas, "Philosophical Reflections on Experimenting with Human Subjects," *Daedalus* 98 (1969): 219–246.

22. William May, "Attitudes Toward the Newly Dead," *Hastings Center Studies* 1 (1973): 6–13.

23. Renée C. Fox and Judith P. Swazey, *The Courage to Fail: A Social View of Organ Transplants and Dialysis* (Chicago: University of Chicago Press, 1978).

24. Blair L. Sadler and Alfred L. Sadler, Jr., "Providing Cadaver Organs: Three Legal Alternatives," *Hastings Center Studies* 1 (1973): 14–26.

25. "Refinements in Criteria for the Determination of Death: An Appraisal: A Report by the Task Force on Death and Dying of the Institute of Society, Ethics and the Life Sciences," *Journal of the American Medical Association* 221 (1972): 48–53.

26. The Hastings Center, "Our Focus Areas." thehastingscenter.org/our-focus-areas/

27. Vanderbilt School of Medicine, Medical Scientist Training Program, "Viven T. Thomas, LLD." medschool.vanderbilt.edu/mstp/person/vivien-t-thomas/

28. Katie McCabe, "Like Something the Lord Made: Vivien Thomas Never Went to College, but He Had a Genius, a Stunning Dexterity. He Might've Been a Great Surgeon. Instead, He Became a Legend." *The Washingtonian* (August 1989).

29. An outstanding review of the friction between organized medicine and organized nursing is provided by Natalie Holt in her essay "'Confusion's Masterpiece': The Development of the Physician Assistant Profession," *Bulletin of the History of Medicine* 72 (1988): 246–278.

30. Thelma Ingles, *Care from the Heart* (BTW Publishing, 2012).

31. Thomas E. Piemme, Alfred M. Sadler, Jr., Reginald D. Carter, and Ruth Ballweg, *The Physician Assistant: An Illustrated History* (Gilbert, AZ: Acacia Publishing, 2013). pahx.org/pa-history-book/

32. Eugene A. Stead, Jr., "Conserving Costly Talents—Providing Physicians New Assistants," *Journal of the American Medical Association* 198 (1966): 1108–9.

33. Henry K. Silver, Loretta C. Ford, and Susan G. Stearly, "A Program to Increase Healthcare for Children: The Pediatric Nurse Practitioner Program," *Pediatrics* 39 (1967): 756–60.

34. Henry K. Silver and John E. Ott, "The Child Health Associate: A New Health Professional to Provide Comprehensive Care to Children," *Pediatrics* 51 (1973): 1–7.

35. Richard Smith, "MEDEX," *Journal of the American Medical Association*, 211 (1970): 1843–1845.

36. Martha Ballenger and Harvey Estes, "Licensure or Responsible Delegation?" *New England Journal of Medicine* 284 (1971): 330–332.

37. Alfred M. Sadler, Jr., Blair L. Sadler, and Ann A. Bliss, *The Physician's Assistant—Today and Tomorrow: Issues Confronting New Health Practitioners, 2nd edition.* (Pensacola, FL: Ballinger, 1975): 93–96. https://pahx.org/wp-content/uploads/2016/11/Sadler_Sadler_Bliss_2nd_Edition.pdf

38. Alfred M. Sadler, Jr., and Blair L. Sadler, "Recent Developments in the Law Relating to the Physician's Assistant." *Vanderbilt Law Review* 24 (1971): 1193–2012.

39. David Keahey and Athena Abdullah, "Physician Assistant Education and Occam's Razor," *Journal of Physician Assistant Education* 28 (2017): S62–S65.

40. Sadler, Sadler, and Bliss, Second edition, Appendix B.

41. Everett M. Rogers, *Diffusion of Innovations, 5th edition.* (New York: Free Press, 2003).

42. Alfred M. Sadler, Jr., Blair L. Sadler, and Ann A. Bliss, *The Physician's Assistant—Today and Tomorrow* (New Haven: Yale University Press, 1972).

43. Alfred M. Sadler, Jr., and Thomas E. Piemme, "Founding of the Association of Physician Assistant Programs and the Organization's Central Role in the Development of the Physician Assistant Profession," *Journal of Physician Assistant Education* 28 (2017): S14–S17.

44. Alfred M. Sadler, Jr., and Thomas E. Piemme, "First Annual Conference on New Health Practitioners," *Journal of Physician Assistant Education* 32 (2021): 90–92.

45. For a detailed account of the development of the PA profession, see the Physician Assistant History Society website (www.pahx.org), and the second edition of *The Physician's Assistant—Today and Tomorrow*, by Alfred M. Sadler, Jr, Blair L. Sadler, and Ann A. Bliss. https://pahx.org/wp-content/uploads/2016/11/Sadler_Sadler_Bliss_2nd_Edition.pdf

46. Sadler, Sadler, and Bliss, Second edition, 135–140.

47. Kristy Thomas, personal communication (2020).

48. Charles Bearden, personal communication (2022).

49. Darrell G. Kirch, "Addressing Healthcare Challenges Through Collaboration," *Journal of Physician Assistant Education* 28 (2017): S5.

50. Eugene Stewart Schneller, *Physician's Assistant: Innovation in the Medical Division of Labour*, (Lexington Books, 1978). (Audible version)

51. Steven R. Covey, *The 7 Habits of Highly Effective People: Restoring the Character Ethic* (New York: Simon & Schuster, 1989).

52. National Academy of Sciences and National Research Council Committee on Trauma; *Accidental Death and Disability: The Neglected Disease of Modern Society.* (Washington, DC: National Academies Press, 1966).

53. C.F. Frey, D.F. Huelke, and P.W. Gikas, "Resuscitation and Survival in Motor Vehicle Accidents," *Journal of Trauma* 9 (1969): 292–310.

54. Matthew L. Edwards, "Race, Policing, and History—Remembering the Freedom House Ambulance Service," *New England Journal of Medicine* 384 (2021): 1386–1389.

55. American Academy of Orthopedic Surgeons, *Emergency Care and Transportation for the Sick and Injured, 11th edition* (Burlington, MA: Jones & Bartlett Learning, 2016).

56. M.A. Farber, "Suddenly Wealthy Johnson Foundation Maps Plans," *New York Times* (May 12, 1972): 43, 53.

57. Alfred M. Sadler, Jr., Blair L. Sadler, and Samuel B. Webb, Jr., *Emergency Medical Care: The Neglected Public Service.* (Cambridge, MA: Ballinger Publishing Co., 1977).

58. Donald Goldman, personal communication (2020).

59. James C. Butler and Susan G. Fowler, "Twenty-Five Years of Emergency Medical Systems: A Retrospective," in *To Improve Health and Health Care, 2000. The Robert Wood Johnson Foundation Anthology* (2000): 253–258.

60. David L. Boyd, "The conceptual development of EMS systems in the United States, Part I," *Emergency Medical Services* 11 (1982): 19–23.

61. Butler and Fowler.

62. Digby Diehl. "A Look Back: The Emergency Medical Services Program," in *To Improve Health and Health Care, 2000. The Robert Wood Johnson Foundation Anthology*, Stephen L. Isaacs & James R. Knickman, eds. (San Francisco: Jossey Bass, 2000): 238.

63. Butler and Fowler.

64. Richard Zuschlag, personal communication (2021).

65. Diehl, 242.

66. Waldemar Nielsen, *The Big Foundations* (New York: Columbia University Press, 1972).

67. M.A. Farber, "Suddenly Wealthy Johnson Foundation Maps Plans," *The New York Times* (May 12, 1972): 43, 53.

68. David E. Rogers, "The President's Statement," The Robert Wood Johnson Foundation Annual Report (1972).

69. Annie Lea Shuster, et al. "An Innovation in Physician Training: The Clinical Scholars Program," *Journal of Medical Education* 58 (1983): 101–111. https://clinicalscholarsnli.org

70. Committee on Emergency Medical Services, Division of Medical Sciences. *Roles And Resources of Federal Agencies in Support of Comprehensive Emergency Systems*. Washington, DC: National Academy of Sciences–National Research Council (March 1972).

71. United Network for Organ Sharing. unos.org

72. Robert D. Truog, Nancy Berlinger, Rachel L. Zacharias, and Mildred Z. Solomon. "Defining Death—Organ Transplantation and the Fifty-Year Legacy of the Harvard Report on Brain Death," *A Hastings Center Special Report* (2018).

73. Uniform Law Commission, Determination of Death Act at uniformlaws.org (1980).

74. American Academy of Neurology, "Update: Determining Brain Death in Adults," *Neurology* 74 (2010): 1911–1918.

75. Thomas A. Nakagawa, Stephen Ashwal, Mudit Mathur, Mohan Mysore; the Society of Critical Care Medicine, Section on Critical Care and Section on Neurology of the American Academy of Pediatrics; and the Child Neurology Society, "Guidelines for the Determination

of Brain Death in Infants and Children: An Update of the 1987 Task Force Recommendations," *Pediatrics* 128 (2011): 720–740.

76. See the National Organ Transplant Act (NOTA; P.L. 98-507), Organ Procurement and Transplantation Network. optn.transplant.hrsa.gov/governance/about-the-optn/

77. D. Goldberg, M. Kallan, et al. "Changing Metrics of Organ Procurement Organization Performance in Order to Increase Organ Donation Rates in the United States," *American Journal of Transplantation* 17 (2017): 3183–3192.

78. US Digital Service, "Executive Summary," *The Costly Effects of an Outdated Organ Donation System* (October 2020).

79. United States Renal Data System. *2018 USRDS Annual Data Report: Epidemiology of Kidney Disease in the United States.* Bethesda, MD: National Institutes of Health, National Institute of Diabetes and Digestive and Kidney Diseases (2018).

80. US Department of Health and Human Services, "The Organ Donation Breakthrough Collaborative: Best Practices Final Report," *Nephrology Nursing Journal: Journal of the American Nephrology Nurses' Association,* 30 (2003): 529–591.

81. Institute for Healthcare Improvement, *The Breakthrough Series: IHI's Collaborative Model for Achieving Breakthrough Improvement.* IHI Innovation Series white paper. Boston: Institute for Healthcare Improvement (2003).

82. David H. Howard, Laura A Siminoff, Virginia McBride, and Monica Lin, "Does Quality Improvement Work? Evaluation of the Organ Donation Breakthrough Collaborative," *Health Services Research* 42 part 1 (2007): 2160–2173.

83. Barry D. Davis, H. James Norton, and David G. Jacobs, "The Organ Donation Breakthrough Collaborative: Has It Made a Difference?" *American Journal of Surgery* 205 (2013): 381–386.

84. Adam Zagorin, "America's Transformative New Organ Donation Rule Goes into Effect Over Objections from Monopolistic Contractors," Project on Government Oversight (April 5, 2021).

85. US Digital Service, *The Costly Effects of an Outdated Organ Donation System* (October 2020). https://bloomworks.digital/organdonationreform

86. House Committee on Oversight and Reform, "Oversight Subcommittee Launches Investigation into Poor Performance, Waste, and Mismanagement in Organ Transplant Industry." Press release (December 23, 2020).

87. National Academies of Sciences, Engineering, and Medicine, 2022 *Realizing the promise of equity in the organ transplantation system*. Washington DC: The National Academies Press. https;//doi.org/10.17226/26364.

88. United States Renal Data System (USRDS), "Healthcare Expenditures for Persons with ESRD."

89. Emily Largent, "NOTA: Not a Good Act for Tissues to Follow," *Quinnipiac Health Law Journal*, 19 (2016): 179–224.

90. Michele Goodwin, ed. *The Global Body Market: Altruism's Limits*. (Cambridge: Cambridge University Press, 2013).

91. John Schiffman and Reade Levinson, "Special Report: U.S. Body Brokers Supply World With Torsos, Limbs And Heads," *Reuters* (February 8, 2018).

92. Sadler, Sadler and Bliss, Second edition, 7–11.

93. Accreditation Review Commission on Education for the Physician Assistant, Inc. (ARC-PA). arc-pa.org

94. National Commission on Certification of Physician Assistants. nccpa .net

95. Where PAs and Physician Associates Can Work Internationally by Stephen Pasquini PA-C. https://www.thepalife.com/physician-assistants -pas-and-associates-around-the-world/

96. *US News*, "Best Health Care Jobs" (2022) https://money.usnews.com/ careers/best-jobs/rankings/best-healthcare-jobs

97. Sadler, Sadler, and Bliss. Second edition, 149–151.

98. American College of Surgeons, *National Trauma Data Bank Annual Report 2016*. Michael C. Chang, Ed., Chicago: American College of Surgeons (2016).

99. American College of Surgeons. "Searching for Verified Trauma Centers." https://www.facs.org/search/trauma-centers

100. Myron L. Weisfeldt, Colleen M. Sitlani, Joseph P. Ornato, et al. "Survival After Application of Automatic External Defibrillators Before Arrival of the Emergency Medical System: Evaluation in the Resuscitation Outcomes Consortium Population of 21 Million," *Journal of American College Cardiology* 55 6 (2010): 1713–20. https://www.jacc .org/doi/abs/10.1016/j.jacc.2009.11.077

101. Ali Watkins, "Rural Ambulance Crews Have Run out of Money and Volunteers," *The New York Times* (April 25, 2021).

102. Benjamin Podsiadlo, "Pandemic Threatens Future of Emergency Medical Services," featured in "In Their Own Words: COVID-19 and the Future of the Healthcare Workforce," *Bill of Health*, Harvard Law (March 17, 2021).

103. American Heart Association, "Cardiac Arrest Survival Greatly Increases When Bystanders Use an Automated External Defibrillator," *Circulation Journal Report* (Jan 26, 2018).

104. *The Hastings Center, Annual Report* (2020): 19. www.thehastings center.org

105. *The Hastings Center Report.* www.thehastingscenter.org

106. The Hastings Center Bioethics Forum. www.thehastingscenter.org ›forum

107. Hastings Center Bioethics Timeline Committee, *The Hastings Center Bioethics Timeline* (2021).

108. Gregory E. Kaebnick and Laura Haupt, Eds. "The Pandemic: Lessons and Questions," *The Hastings Center Special Report* 50 (2020): 3.

109. Carol Levine, "Bioethics, Nazi Analogies, and the Coronavirus Pandemic," Bioethics Forum, *The Hastings Center* (Dec 7, 2020).

110. Barron H. Lerner, "Resisting Public Health Measures, Then and Now," *The Hastings Center* (Dec 2, 2020).

111. Elliott Davis, "These 10 Countries Are Seen to Have the Best Public Health Care Systems: Amid the COVID-19 Pandemic, Western European Countries Top a List of Nations Seen to Have Strong Healthcare," *US News & World Report* (Apr 13, 2021).

112. Eric C. Schneider, et al. Mirror, Mirror 2021: Reflecting Poorly: Health Care in the U.S. Compared to Other High-Income Countries. *Commonwealth Fund* (Aug 2021).

113. Steffie Woolhandler, Terry Campbell, and David U. Himmelstein, "Costs of Healthcare Administration in the United States and Canada," *New England Journal of Medicine* 349 (2003): 768–775.

114. Mona Hanna-Attisha, *What the Eyes Don't See: A Story of Crisis, Resistance, and Hope in an American City* (London: One World, 2019).

115. Josh Karliner, Sonia Roschnik, Richard Boyd, Ben Ashby, Kristian Steele, and Renzo Guinto, Global Roadmap for Health Care Decarbonization. *Health Care Without Harm* (2021). https://healthcareclimate action.org/roadmap

116. Mamie Till-Mobley and Christopher Benson, *Death of Innocence: The Story of the Hate Crime That Changed America* (New York: One World, 2004).

117. Candace Lightner, *Giving Sorrow Words* (New York: Grand Central Publishing, 1991).

118. Julia Hallisy and Helen Haskell, "Empowered Patient Hospital Guide for Patients and Families." The Empowered Patient Coalition. www.empoweredpatientcoalition.org

119. This phrasing is borrowed from Boston Philharmonic Orchestra conductor Benjamin Zander, as used in his book *The Art of Possibility: Transforming Professional and Personal Life,* coauthored with Rosamund Zander (New York: Penguin Books, 2000).

120. Shirley Chisholm, *Unbought and Unbossed,* 40th edition (Charlotte, NC: Take Root Media, 2010).

121. Amanda Gorman. The Hill We Climb: An Inaugural Poem for the Country (New York: Viking Books for Young Readers, 2021).

122. Gerald G. May, Addiction and *Grace: Love and Spirituality in the Healing of Addictions* (New York: Harper Collins, 1991).

123. Sam Quinones, Dreamland: *The True Tale of America's Opiate Epidemic* (New York: Bloomsbury, 2015).

124. Richard Rohr, *Breathing Under Water: Spirituality and the Twelve Steps* (Cincinnati: Franciscan Media. 2011).

125. Blair L. Sadler and Kevin Stewart, "Leading in a Crisis: The Power of Transparency" (*The Health Foundation,* December 2015): 1–27.

126. Blair L. Sadler, Leonard L. Berry, Robin Guenther, D. Kirk Hamilton, et al. "Fable Hospital 2.0: The Business Case for Building Better Health Care Facilities," *Hastings Center Report,* 41, no.1 (2011): 13–23.

127. Blair L. Sadler and Robin Guenther, "Ten Rules for 21st Century Healthcare: A US Perspective on Creating Healthy, Healing Environments," *Future Hospital Journal,* vol.2, no. 1 (2015): 1–6.

128. B. Sadler, D. Payne, N. Kini, P. Kurtin, and C. Dobies, "Behind the Scenes of a Collaborative: The Child health Accountability Initiative, a Rapid-Improvement Collaborative for Pediatrics," *Health Forum Journal* (November/December 2001): 58–59.

129. Blair L. Sadler, "To the Class of 2005: Will You Be Ready for the Quality Revolution?" *Joint Commission Journal on Quality and Patient Safety* 32:1 (January 2006): 51–55.

130. Blair L. Sadler, Review, "Why Health Care is Going Green," *Hastings Center Report,* 45, no.4, (July-August 2015).

131. Blair L. Sadler, "How a Children's Hospital Discovered Child Pornographers in Its Midst," *Health Affairs,* vol 30, no.9 (September 2011): 1795–1798.

132. Carole Jenny, "Preventing the Exploitation and Abuse of Children," *Health Affairs* (April 2012): 883.

133. Blair L. Sadler, "The Ethical Imperative: More Important Than Ever," *The Rady Business Journal,* (Winter 2013).

134. Göran Henriks, Blair L. Sadler, and Pedro Delgado, "Leadership Lessons: From Sports to Health Care," *IHI National Forum* (2015): 6.

135 Alfred M. Sadler, Jr. and Blair L. Sadler, "Organ Transplantation and the Uniform Anatomical Gift Act: A Fifty-Year Perspective," *Uniform Law Commission* (2018) https://www.uniformlaws.org/blogs/katie-robinson/2018/12/06/50th-anniversary-of-the-uniform-anatomical-gift-ac

136. Blair L. Sadler and Alfred M. Sadler, Jr. "Organ Transplantation and the Uniform Anatomical Gift Act: A Fifty-Year Perspective," *Hastings Center Report* 48 (2018): 4.

137. Alfred M. Sadler, Jr., and Blair L. Sadler, "Organ Donation and Transplantation in the US: 50 Years of Success, Strategies for Improvement," The Hastings Center Bioethics Forum. (2018)

138. Blair L. Sadler and Alfred M. Sadler, Jr. "Is an Opt-Out System Likely to Increase Organ Donation?" *British Medical Journal* 364 (2019): 392–393.

Suggested Reading

Books and Major Reports

Arnold, J., *Raising Our Hands: How White Women Can Stop Avoiding Hard Conversations, Start Accepting Responsibility, and Find Our Place in the New Frontlines*. Dallas: BenBella Books, Inc., 2020.

Assaiante, P. and J. Zug. *Run to the Roar: Coaching to Overcome Fear*, New York: Portfolio Penguin, 2010.

Bate, P., P. Mendel, and G. Robert. "The Art, Science, and Sociology of Improvement: San Diego Children's Hospital," in *Organizing for Quality: The Improvement Journeys of Leading Hospitals in Europe and the United States*. Abingdon, Oxon, UK: Radcliffe Publishing, 2010.

Berlinger, N. *After Harm: Medical Error and the Ethics of Forgiveness*. Baltimore: Johns Hopkins UP, 2005.

Berwick, D. *Escape Fire: Designs for the Future of Healthcare: Collected Speeches 1992–2002*. San Francisco: Jossey-Bass, 2004.

Berwick, D. *Promising Care: How We Can Rescue Healthcare by Improving It: Collected Speeches 2003–2012*, San Francisco: Jossey-Bass, 2014.

Berry, L. and K. Seltman. *Management Lessons from Mayo Clinic: Inside One of the Most Admired Service Organizations*. New York: McGraw Hill, 2008.

Berry, L. *Discovering the Soul of Service*. New York: Free Press, 1999.

Bisognano, M. and C. Kenney. *Pursuing the Triple Aim: Seven Innovators Show the Way to Better Care, Better Health, and Lower Costs*. San Francisco: Jossey-Bass, 2012.

Brown, B. *Daring Greatly: How the Courage to be Vulnerable Transforms the Way We Live, Love, Parent and Lead*. New York: Avery, 2012.

Buettner, D. The Blue Zones Challenge, *National Geographic*, 2021. bluezones.co

Butler C., and S. Fowler. "Twenty-Five Years of Emergency Medical Systems: A Retrospective," in *To Improve Health and Health Care 2000. The*

Robert Wood Johnson Foundation Anthology, S. Isaacs & J. Knickman, Eds. San Francisco: Jossey-Bass, 2000. 253–258.

Callahan, D. *What Kind of Life? The Limits of Medical* Progress. Washington, DC: Georgetown University Press, 1995.

Callahan, D. *In Search of the Good: A Life in Bioethics.* Cambridge, MA: MIT Press, 2012.

Campbell, Joseph. *The Hero with a Thousand Faces.* New York: Pantheon Books, 1949.

Covey, S. *The 7 Habits of Highly Effective People: Restoring the Character Ethic.* New York: Simon & Schuster, 1989.

Crisp, N. *24 Hours to Save the NHS*, Oxford: Oxford UP, 2011.

Crisp, N. *Health is Made at Home, Hospitals are for Repairs: Building a Healthy and Health-Creating Society* (SALUS Global Knowledge Exchange, 2020).

Diehl, D. "A Look Back: The Emergency Medical Services Program," in *To Improve Health and Health Care 2000. The Robert Wood Johnson Foundation Anthology*, S. Isaacs & J. Knickman, Eds. San Francisco: Jossey-Bass, 2000.

Edmondson, A. *The Fearless Organization: Creating Psychological Safety in the Workplace for Learning, Innovation, and Growth.* Hoboken, NJ: John Wiley & Sons, 2018.

Fox, R., and J. Swazey. *The Courage to Fail: A Social View of Organ Transplants and Dialysis.* Chicago: University of Chicago Press, 1978.

Frankel, V. *The Unheard Cry for Meaning: Psychotherapy and Humanism.* New York: Simon and Schuster, 1978.

Franklin, B. *Poor Richard's Almanac.* Mount Vernon, N.Y:Peter Pauper Press, 1980

Gardner, J. *On Leadership.* New York: The Free Press, 1990.

Garland, L. and A. Buss. *Hear Here: Effective Communication - Engaging With Our Aware Loving Heart.* Amazon, 2022.

Gaylin, W. *In the Service of Their Country: War Resisters in Prison.* New York: Viking Press, 1970.

Gladwell, M. *The Tipping Point: How Little Things Can Make a Big Difference.* New York: Back Bay Books, 2002.

Kabat-Zinn, J. *Full Catastrophic Living: Using the Wisdom of Your Body and Mind to Face Stress, Pain, and Illness.* New York: Bantam Dell, 2005.

Ingles, T., S. Haradon, V.I. Haradon, and P. Wheeldon. *Care from the Heart: Memoirs of the Remarkable Woman and Pioneering Nurse who Helped Inspire the Duke University Physician Assistant Program and Nursing around the World.* La Mesa, CA: BTW Publishing, 2012.

Institute of Medicine. *Organ Donation: Opportunities for Action.* J. Childress and C. Liverman, eds. Washington, DC: The National Academies Press, 2006.

JAAPA and JPAE. *The PA Profession: 50 Years and Counting.* 2017. http://bit. ly/znoAell (ebook available at pahx.org)

Katz, J. A.M. Capron, and E.S. Glass. *Experimentation with Human Beings: The Authority of the Investigator, Subject, Profession, and State in the Human Experimentation Process.* New York: Russell Sage Foundation, 1972.

Kayingo, G. and V. Hass, V., eds. *The Health Professions Educator: A Practical Guide for New and Established Faculty.* New York: Springer Publishing Co., 2018.

Levinson, D., with C. Darrow, E. Klein, and M. Levinson. *Seasons of a Man's Life.* New York: Random House, 1978.

Lippard, V. and Purcell, E., eds., *Intermediate Level Health Practitioners*, Josiah Macy, Jr., Foundation, New York, 1973.

Lysaught, J. *An Abstract for Action: Report of the National Commission for the Study of Nursing and Nursing Education.* New York: McGraw-Hill, 1970.

National Academies of Sciences, Engineering, and Medicine; Health and Medicine Division; Board on Health Sciences Policy; Committee on Issues in Organ Donor Intervention Research. *Opportunities for Organ Donor Intervention Research: Saving Lives by Improving the Quality and Quantity of Organs for Transplantation.* Washington, DC: National Academies Press, 2017.

National Academy of Sciences and National Research Council Committee on Trauma; *Accidental Death and Disability: The Neglected Disease of Modern Society.* Washington, DC: National Academies Press, 1966.

National Conference on Uniform State Laws. *The Uniform Determination of Death Act*, 1980.

Peck, S. *The Road Less Traveled: A New Psychology of Love, Traditional Values and Spiritual Growth.* New York: Simon & Schuster, 1978.

Physician Assistants as Social Innovators in Healthcare. Physician Assistant History Society, Inc.; 2022. https://pahx.org/pa-history-book/

President's Commission for the Study of Ethical Problems in Medicine and Biomedical and Behavioral Research, *Defining Death: Medical, Legal and Ethical Issues in the Determination of Death.* Washington DC: US Government Printing Office, 1981.

Record, J. *Staffing Primary Care in 1990: Physician Replacement and Cost Savings.* New York: Springer Publishing, 1981.

Schneller, E. *The Physician's Assistant: Innovation in the Medical Division of Labor*, Lexington Books, 1978.

Schweitzer, A. *Out of My Life and Thought: An Autobiography.* 60th Anniversary Edition [*Aus meinem Leben und Denken.*] Antje Bultmann Lemke, translator. Baltimore: Johns Hopkins University Press, 2009. P. I 147.

Suzuki, S. and T. Dixon. *Zen Mind, Beginner's Mind*. New York: Walker/Weatherhill, 1970.

Thompson, J., *Lead True, Live Your Values, Build Your People, Inspire Your Community*. Charleston, SC: Forbes Books, 2017.

Truog, R., N. Berlinger, R. Zacharias, and M. Solomon, eds. "Defining Death: Organ Transplantation and the Fifty-Year Legacy of the Harvard Report on Brain Death." *The Hastings Center Report* 48, 2018.

Tye, J. and B. Dent. *Building a Culture of Ownership in Healthcare: The Invisible Architecture of Core Values, Attitude, and Self Empowerment 2d ed*, New Jersey, Spencer Publishing, 2018.

Weill, D. *Exhale: Hope, Healing and a Life in Transplant*. A Post Hill Press Book, 2021.

Wijesinghe, S. *101 Primary Care Case Studies*. Springer Publishing 2020. Zander, R. and B. Zander. *The Art of Possibility: Transforming Professional and Personal Life*. Boston: Harvard Business School Press, 2000.

Zarbock, S. and K. Harbart, eds. *Physician Assistants: Present and Future Models of Utilization*. New York: Praeger Publishers, 1986.

Articles and DVDs

Ballweg, R., W. Stanhope., A. Sadler, and T. Piemme. "The Way We Were," *DVD* available through the Physician Assistant History Society, Johns Creek, GA 30097 (2012). pahx.org

Beecher, H.K. "Ethical Problems Created by the Hopelessly Unconscious Patient," *New England Journal of Medicine* 278 (1968): 1425–1430.

Bodenheimer, T. and C. Sinsky. "From the Triple Aim to the Quadruple Aim, Care of the Patient Requires Care of the Provider." *Annals of Family Medicine*. 12(6) (2014): 573–576.

Caplan, A. "Death: An Evolving, Normative Concept," in *Defining Death: Organ Transplantation and the Fifty-Year Legacy of the Harvard Report on Brain Death* Special report, *The Hastings Center Report* 48 (2018): S60–S62.

Capron, A. "Beecher *Dépassé*. Fifty Years of Determining Death Legally," in *Defining Death: Organ Transplantation and the Fifty-Year Legacy of the Harvard Report on Brain Death* Special report, *The Hastings Center Report* 48 (2018): S14–S18.

Carter, R., R. Ballweg, and L. Konopka-Sauer. "Preserving 50 Years of Physician Assistant History," *Journal of Physician Assistant Education* 28 (2017): S85–S89.

Cawley, J. and R. Dehn. "Physician Assistant Educational Research: 50 Years On," *Journal of Physician Assistant Education* 28 (2017): S56–61.

Ford, L.C. "Reflections on 50 years of Change," *Journal of the American Association of Nurse Practitioners* 27 (2015): 294–295.

Jones, E. and J. Houchins. "Physician Assistant Contributions to Medical and Higher Education," *Journal of Physician Assistant Education* 28 (2017): S71–S74.

Komaroff, A., W.L. Black, M. Flatley, et al. "Protocols for Physicians Assistants–Management of Diabetes and Hypertension," *New England Journal of Medicine* 290 (1974): 307–319.

Matsumoto, E. "History of Nurse Practitioner Profession, Loretta Ford Interview" DVD (2016) available at www.ebay.com.

Piemme, T. and A. Sadler. "The Physician Assistant: A Respected and Unique Brand." *PA Professional Journal* (2012): 26–27.

Piemme, T. and A. Sadler. "The Vagabond Apostrophe." *PA Professional Journal* (2012): 51–53.

Sadler, A. "Physician Assistants in the United States–Lessons Learned," *Journal of the Japanese Surgical Society* (2015): 116:201–2014

Sadler, A. "Collaborating with PA's for more than 48 years," *Journal of the American Academy of Physician Assistants* 30 (2017): 8–10.

Sadler, A. and A. Davis. "How PAs became licensed to practice in the United States," *Journal of the American Academy of Physician Assistants* 30 (2017): 46–49.

Sadler, A. "Optimal Team Practice: How to Get There," *Journal of the American Academy of Physician Assistants,* 30 (2017): 8–9.

Sadler, B. and N.R. Sadler. "Having Conversations about Organ Donation," *The Hastings Center Report* 45 (2015): 49.

Sadler B. "How a Children's Hospital Discovered Child Pornographers in its Midst," *Health Affairs* 30 (2011): 1795–1798.

Sadler, B. "To the Class of 2005: Will You Be Ready for the Quality Revolution?" *Joint Commission Journal on Quality and Patient Safety* 32 (2006): 51–55.

Sadler, B. and A Sadler. "Can Social Media Increase Transplant Donation and Save Lives?" Bioethics Forum Blog, The Hastings Center, August 24, 2012.

Sadler, B. and R. Guenther. "Ten Rules for 21st Century Healthcare: A US Perspective on Creating Healthy, Healing Environments," *Future Hospital Journal* 2 (2015): 22–27.

Sadler, B., L.L. Berry, R. Guenther, D.K. Hamilton, et al. "Fable Hospital 2.0: The Business Case for Building Better Healthcare Facilities," *Hastings Center Report* 41 (2011): 13–23.

Sadler B. and K. Stewart. *Leading in a Crisis: The Power of Transparency.* London: The Health Foundation (2015).

Sox, H. and R. Tompkins. "The Training of Physician's Assistants: The Use of the Clinical Algorithm System for Patient Care, Audit of Performance and Education." *New England Journal of Medicine*, 288 (1973): 818–824.

Truog, R. "Lessons from the Case of Jahi McMath," in *Defining Death: Organ Transplantation and the Fifty-Year Legacy of the Harvard Report on Brain Death, The Hastings Center Report* 48 (2018): S70–S73.

Websites

Accreditation Review Commission on Education for the Physician Assistant, Inc.
arc-pa.org

American Academy of Pediatrics
aap.org

American Academy of Physician Associates (physician associates and physician assistants)
aapa.org

American Association of Nurse Practitioners
aanp.org

American College of Emergency Physicians
acep.org

American College of Physicians
acponline.org

American College of Surgeons
facs.org

American Medical Association
ama-assn.org

American Society of Transplantation
myast.org

American Society of Transplant Surgeons
asts.org

Association of American Medical Colleges
aamc.org

Breakthrough for Men
breakthroughformen.org

Donate Life America
donatelife.net

Hastings Center
Hastingscenter.org

Health Care Without Harm
hcwh.org

Institute for Healthcare Improvement
ihi.org

National Academy of Medicine
nam.edu

National Commission on Certification of Physician Assistants
nccpa.net

National League for Nursing
nln.org

Organ Procurement and Transplant Network
optn.transplant.hrsa.gov

ORGANIZE
organize.org

Physician Assistant Education Association
paeaonline.org

Physician Assistant History Society
pahx.org

Scientific Registry of Transplant Recipients
srtr.org

STOP THE BLEED®
stopthebleed.org

Toastmasters International
toastmasters.org

United Network for Organ Sharing
unos.org

Acknowledgments

We were very fortunate to benefit from the wisdom, generosity, and ideas of many people before, during, and after our work together.

When we first decided to explore our idea of working as a medical-legal team, four people played instrumental roles in helping us decide that our vision was realistic. They opened the doors that made it all possible. Paul Russell, chairman of surgery, provided the opportunity at Massachusetts General Hospital for us to depart from traditional grand rounds and discuss the legal and ethical issues underpinning the Good Samaritan problem. Anthony Amsterdam of the University of Pennsylvania Law School critically reviewed our draft position paper and encouraged us to pursue without delay our idea of collaboration. Luther Terry, the vice president of health affairs at the University of Pennsylvania and the former surgeon general, strongly encouraged us to act on our ideas and opened doors to the top echelons at the NIH and HEW to pursue them. John Sherman, associate director at NIH, broke the logjam holding up our applications to join the institutes. Without the guidance and support of these four visionary leaders, our idea would probably have remained just an idea.

At NIH, Joseph Murtaugh was an outstanding first chief and mentor. We will always remember his opening words: "Gentlemen, we have a problem." Our first assignment, to review all the laws relating to organ and tissue donation, set us on a life-changing course.

Blythe Stason, the former University of Michigan Law School dean and chair of the Uniform Law Commission committee drafting a new model state law on organ and tissue donation, included us in his thinking and invited us to be his consultants and collaborators in drafting the Uniform Anatomical Gift Act.

Numerous institute directors and leaders at NIH supported our work, including Donald Whedon, Kenneth Endicott, Theodore Cooper, Jesse Steinfeld, and Jack Masur. Robert Stevenson invited us to participate in the Committee on Organ Transplantation of the National Academy of Sciences.

We were most fortunate to have two private luncheons with Chief Justice Earl Warren at the Supreme Court. His encouragement about our work was galvanizing. His description of his strategies to achieve a unanimous opinion in *Brown v. Board of Education* was a priceless lesson in finding common ground.

Daniel Callahan and Willard Gaylin were generous and courageous trailblazers in creating The Hastings Center and including us in their early discussions of the emerging field of bioethics. Our enhanced understanding and appreciation for the core values underlying social issues has proved invaluable.

As assistant secretary for health, Roger Egeberg provided us with the opportunity to review and develop recommendations for the licensure and certification of new health personnel at a time when the nation was facing a severe health manpower shortage. Thomas Hatch ran the nation's allied health manpower programs, and Douglas Fenderson was a leader in the research and analysis of various healthcare models. Both provided essential context and pointed us to key people and places to explore.

We had the benefit of comprehensive site visits and discussions with pioneers in new health practitioner programs: Eugene Stead and Thelma Ingles at Duke, Henry Silver and Loretta Ford in Colorado, and Richard Smith in Seattle. Harvey Estes and Martha Ballenger at Duke helped us land on a straightforward way to legally approve physician assistants, designing a concise amendment to the state medical practice acts without creating a new licensure law.

At the invitation of Jack Cole, we joined the Yale University School of Medicine faculty to lead the newly formed Yale Trauma Program and to create the Yale Physician Assistant Program in collaboration with Paul Moson and Ann Bliss. Samuel Webb was an effective faculty colleague in conducting the comprehensive study of emergency medical services in Connecticut. The medical school faculty provided excellent teaching and curriculum support for our new physician assistant program.

Our work in developing the physician assistant field also benefited from the support of John Hubbard and Barbara Andrew at the National Board of Medical Examiners, and Edmund Pellegrino, who chaired their study committee and had been an advisor to our work on organ transplantation. Thomas Piemme was an invaluable colleague over forty-five years.

At the Robert Wood Johnson Foundation, David Rogers was a superb leader and assembled a remarkably diverse array of full and part-time staff to accomplish great things in a short time. Walsh McDermott, Margaret Mahoney, Terrance Keenan, Robert Blendon, and Frank Karel contributed thoughtful and skillful ideas and experience to the foundation. Taking the Connecticut EMS model to national scale was a remarkable opportunity that benefited from the foundation's strategic advice and collaboration. Calvin Bland and David Cusic ably helped manage the RWJ national EMS program.

We are very grateful to Donald Berwick for his thoughtful and compelling foreword to our book. In writing this book, we have enjoyed working with Atiya Dwyer and Joseph DiNucci at Silicon Valley Press. Cheryl Dumesnil, Henry Ferris, and Marly Cornell have provided invaluable and generous editorial advice and assistance.

We thank the several people who read all or parts of earlier drafts of this book, including Charles Bearden, Laurence Beck, Leonard Berry, Calvin Bland, Robert Blendon, Alex Capron, Joseph Fins, Donald Goldman, Lee Jampolski, Gerald Kayingo, David Lawrence, Megan Mayer, Nick Rizopolous, and Millie Solomon.

Subject Index

Name Index

About the Authors

Alfred Sadler, MD FACP, ScD (Hon) co-founded the Physician Assistant Program at California State University Monterey Bay in 2015. Trained in surgery at the Hospital of the University of Pennsylvania and in internal medicine at the Harvard Medical School and the  Massachusetts General Hospital, he practiced primary care in Monterey County for nearly forty years with emphasis on compassionate care for underserved populations. He served as the first President of the Physician Assistant Education Society and as President of the Physician Assistant History Society.

Blair Sadler, JD is a Senior Fellow at the Institute for Healthcare Improvement (IHI) and a faculty member at the UCSD Rady School of Management, where he teaches about leading with transparency and empathy in times of crisis. A graduate of the University of Pennsylvania  Law School, he served as a law clerk for two judges of the Superior Court of Pennsylvania. From 1980 to 2006, he was the president & CEO of Rady Children's Hospital in San Diego. He serves on the boards of The Hastings Center, Healthcare Without Harm, and the Access Youth Academy.